Why Worry About Future Generations?

UEHIRO SERIES IN PRACTICAL ETHICS

General Editor: Julian Savulescu, University of Oxford

Choosing Children
The Ethical Dilemmas of Genetic Intervention
Jonathan Glover

Messy Morality
The Challenge of Politics
C. A. J. Coady

Killing in War
Jeff McMahan

Beyond Humanity?
The Ethics of Biomedical Enhancement
Allen Buchanan

Ethics for Enemies
Terror, Torture, and War
F. M. Kamm

Unfit for the Future
The Need for Moral Enhancement
Ingmar Persson and Julian Savulescu

The Robust Demands of the Good
Ethics with Attachment, Virtue, and Respect
Philip Pettit

Why Does Inequality Matter?
T. M. Scanlon

Why Worry About Future Generations?
Samuel Scheffler

Fellow Creatures
Our Obligations to the Other Animals
Christine M. Korsgaard

WHY WORRY ABOUT FUTURE GENERATIONS?

SAMUEL SCHEFFLER

UNIVERSITY PRESS

Great Clarendon Street, Oxford, OX2 6DP,
United Kingdom

Oxford University Press is a department of the University of Oxford.
It furthers the University's objective of excellence in research, scholarship,
and education by publishing worldwide. Oxford is a registered trade mark of
Oxford University Press in the UK and in certain other countries

© Samuel Scheffler 2018

The moral rights of the author have been asserted

First Edition published in 2018

All rights reserved. No part of this publication may be reproduced, stored in
a retrieval system, or transmitted, in any form or by any means, without the
prior permission in writing of Oxford University Press, or as expressly permitted
by law, by licence or under terms agreed with the appropriate reprographics
rights organization. Enquiries concerning reproduction outside the scope of the
above should be sent to the Rights Department, Oxford University Press, at the
address above

You must not circulate this work in any other form
and you must impose this same condition on any acquirer

Published in the United States of America by Oxford University Press
198 Madison Avenue, New York, NY 10016, United States of America

British Library Cataloguing in Publication Data
Data available

Library of Congress Control Number: 2017956920

ISBN 978-0-19-879898-9

Links to third party websites are provided by Oxford in good faith and
for information only. Oxford disclaims any responsibility for the materials
contained in any third party website referenced in this work.

CONTENTS

Acknowledgments vii

1 Temporal Parochialism and Its Discontents 1
2 Reasons to Worry: Interest and Love 40
3 Reasons to Worry: Valuation and Reciprocity 68
4 Attachment and Axiology 87
5 Conservatism, Temporal Bias, and Future Generations 105

Bibliography 137
Index 145

ACKNOWLEDGMENTS

This short book is based on the Uehiro Lectures that I delivered at Oxford University in January, 2016. I am grateful to Julian Savulescu and his colleagues at the Oxford Uehiro Centre for Practical Ethics for inviting me to deliver the lectures and for their warm hospitality during my visit. I am also indebted to the participants in the discussions that followed the lectures for their stimulating questions and comments. Questions from Jeff McMahan and Janet Radcliffe Richards were especially helpful and prompted significant changes when I was revising the lectures for publication.

The ideas developed here have their origin in a brief talk that I gave in 2013 under the auspices of the Princeton Institute for International and Regional Studies, and I am grateful to Melissa Lane and Robert Socolow for the invitation to give that talk. In the course of preparing the Uehiro Lectures for delivery and then later of revising them for publication, I had the opportunity to present portions of my work in progress to a number of different audiences. These presentations included the Raymond West Memorial Lecture at Stanford in 2015, the Spring 2015 David Norton Memorial Lecture at the University of Delaware, a keynote lecture at the Braga Meetings on Ethical and Political Philosophy at the University of Minho in 2015, the Jerome Simon Lectures at the University of Toronto in 2016, and the keynote lecture at the Speculative Ethics Forum at St. John's University in 2016. I benefited greatly from audience discussion on all these occasions.

Drafts of some or all of this material were also discussed in graduate seminars that I taught at NYU in 2014 and 2016, and a late draft of the manuscript as a whole was the focus of a workshop organized by Jay Wallace under the auspices of the Einstein Ethics Group in Berlin in 2017. I am grateful to the participants in the NYU seminars and the Berlin workshop for their many critical and constructive contributions.

In addition, I am indebted to a number of individuals for providing me with written comments on one version or another of the draft manuscript. Niko Kolodny, Dale Jamieson, Jed Lewinsohn, Jake Nebel, Derek Parfit, Peter Unger, and Jay Wallace all provided extremely valuable comments, as did three readers for Oxford University Press, one of whom remains anonymous but two of whom—David Brink and Jeff McMahan—were willing to relinquish their anonymity. Whatever its remaining flaws and limitations, this book has been much improved thanks to the generous assistance of all these people.

Samuel Scheffler

New York
August 2017

CHAPTER ONE

Temporal Parochialism and Its Discontents

In this book I want to explore, in a frankly speculative spirit, some questions about our attitudes toward future generations. I hope that you will excuse the speculative character of my remarks. The questions I want to consider are large and difficult to think about, but they are important and perhaps even urgent, and I don't believe that they have received as much attention from philosophers as they deserve.

With the notable exceptions of Burkean conservatives and the adherents of some religious traditions, most of us who live in contemporary liberal societies lack a rich set of evaluative resources for thinking about the human beings who will come after us. We do not have a highly developed set of ideas about the value of human continuity, or about the values we hope will be realized in the future, or about the values and norms that should inform our own activities insofar as they affect future generations or depend on the expectation that there will be future generations. People's hopes or fears about the fate of their own personal descendants—primarily their children and grandchildren—constitute a partial exception to this generalization, but even these hopes and fears are usually fairly vague and inchoate. They are often limited to a general desire that things will go well for their descendants and an anxiety that they won't. Beyond that, many people are vaguely uneasy about the impact of our way of life on future generations, and there are the familiar ritualized declarations by public officials about our responsibilities to those who come after us. These declarations are sometimes transparently opportunistic, but even when they are sincere, they rarely spell out the content of the alleged responsibilities in a clear and convincing way.

To some extent, the poverty of our evaluative discourse about the human future is matched by the poverty of our discourse about the human past. It is not just that levels of historical literacy are low. Perhaps that has always been true. It is also that, in recent times, a number of intellectual tendencies have combined to erode our disposition to look back on our forebears with reverence or piety or to see them as setting standards to which we are bound by ideals of loyalty or honor to adhere. Among these intellectual tendencies I would include tendencies toward individualism and religious skepticism, as well as an increased appreciation of cultural diversity and a simultaneous discomfort about the moral ambiguity of national and ethnic affiliations. These tendencies have helped to undermine earlier conceptions of the normative significance of the past, and we have not yet developed another set of concepts and attitudes to replace those whose grip on us has loosened.

There is an interesting contrast, I think, between the way we think about temporal periods other than our own and the way we think about regions of the Earth other than our own. "Globalization" and "global integration" are among the great buzzwords of our age. It is a familiar fact that technological advances have facilitated dramatic increases in global travel and communication, and in so doing have made possible social and economic interaction across national borders on an unprecedented scale. This in turn has had far-reaching effects on the way that many people understand the social world and their own place in it. And it has created increasing pressure to develop transnational norms and institutions to structure and regulate global travel, communications, commerce, and finance. So there has been a rapidly growing interest, both within the academy and outside it, in what might be called "global normativity": in topics like cosmopolitanism, global justice, human rights, and international law.

Yet even as we are becoming, so to speak, geographically more cosmopolitan, we have become temporally more parochial: more firmly rooted in our own time, less likely to see our relations to those who came before us and those who will come after us as governed by a rich set of values and norms. We talk a great deal about global or international integration, but very little about temporal or intergenerational integration. Our awareness of the multiple interconnections among people in different parts of the world continues to expand, but our sense of the connections among different human generations has become increasingly impoverished, as compared, say, with more traditional societies, which often had rich and vivid conceptions of the importance of *ancestors* and *descendants* and of the continuity of the generations.

Up to this point, I have been allowing myself to speak freely about what *we* think and about *our* attitudes and beliefs. This uninhibited use of the first-person plural may strike some readers as lazy or presumptuous: a cheap linguistic device for passing off armchair speculations as universal truths. But my pronominal choice reflects no universalist ambition. In speaking of *our* attitudes, I am not suggesting that these are everyone's attitudes nor do I presume that they are the attitudes of the reader. My choice of terminology has a different motivation. On the one hand, my use of the first-person *plural* is meant to indicate that I do not take myself merely to be describing my own idiosyncratic attitudes. I am instead trying to characterize patterns of belief that I hope readers will recognize as constituting familiar (even if not universal) tendencies within contemporary thought and discourse. On the other hand, my use of the *first-person* plural is meant to emphasize that, when I suggest deficiencies or tensions in those patterns of thought, I do not mean to exempt myself from the criticism.[1]

The changes of attitude that I have been describing have not taken place overnight. More than seventy years ago, T.S. Eliot described the emergence of what he regarded as a new kind of provincialism, "the provincialism, not of space, but of time."[2] Eliot was a cultural conservative and his primary concern, in speaking about the provincialism of time, was with what he saw as his contemporaries' inadequate appreciation of the values and standards

---

[1] In *Death and the Afterlife* (New York: Oxford University Press, 2013, at pp. 17–18), I explained my use of the first-person plural in that book by quoting a passage from an article by David Lewis. Here let me instead quote some suggestive remarks of Bernard Williams's in his *Shame and Necessity* (Berkeley: University of California Press, 1993, at p. 171):

> More than one friend, reading this book in an earlier version, has asked who this ubiquitous "we" represents. It refers to people in a certain cultural situation, but who is in that situation? Obviously it cannot mean everybody in the world, or everybody in the West. I hope it does not mean only people who already think as I do. The best I can say is that "we" operates not through a previously fixed designation, but through invitation. (The same is true, I believe, of "we" in much philosophy, and particularly in ethics.) It is not a matter of "I" telling "you" what I and others think, but of my asking you to consider to what extent you and I think some things and perhaps need to think others.

[2] T.S. Eliot, *What is a Classic?* (London: Faber and Faber, 1944), p. 30. The provincialism he had in mind was a provincialism for which "history is merely the chronicle of human devices which have served their turn and been scrapped, one for which the world is solely the property of the living, a property in which the dead hold no shares."

of the past. But it is possible to interpret the attitudes that elicited his concern as symptoms of the more general phenomenon that I am calling our temporal parochialism, which includes our attitudes both toward the past and toward the future.

It is natural to wonder why our temporal parochialism should be increasing even as its geographical analogue has been declining. The explanation may at first seem straightforward. As I have already noted, recent decades have seen dramatic increases in global travel, communications, and economic activity, and our growing cosmopolitanism has been largely a response to those facts. But there have, of course, been no comparable temporal developments: no increases in travel or communications or economic exchange across different temporal periods. Moreover, many of us no longer hold the traditional beliefs that in earlier times underwrote people's sense of the connections among the generations. We do not find credible the stories that made it possible for people to assign such significance to their relations with their ancestors and descendants, and to see the generations as being so closely bound together. Viewed in this light, it may not seem surprising that we have become temporally more parochial even as we have become geographically more cosmopolitan.[3] These divergent tendencies may

---

[3] It may be said that the contrast between our geographical cosmopolitanism and our temporal parochialism is imperfect, because the term "cosmopolitanism" is really a misnomer. Our so-called cosmopolitanism is really a stance we take toward our fellow earthlings and not toward the cosmos as a whole. If there were human beings scattered throughout the universe, and we had the capacity to interact with them, then the true extent of our spatial or geographical cosmopolitanism would be put to the test. As things stand, however, the increase in our so-called cosmopolitanism may amount to little more than the substitution of a wider parochialism for a narrower one: a parochialism of the planet for a parochialism of the nation

even have a common cause, inasmuch as both of them have been encouraged by the rise of modern science. On the one hand, science has helped to facilitate the rapidly growing connections among the people of the world that have fueled the tendency toward geographical cosmopolitanism. On the other hand, science has helped to undermine many of the myths and narratives that sustained the confidence of traditional societies in the bonds linking them to other generations.

Still, there are other possible explanations of our divergent attitudes that are also worth considering.[4] One of these involves changing beliefs about the metaphysics of time. Perhaps we have become

or the tribe. Yet even if our cosmopolitanism, as I will continue to call it, really does amount to a wider form of parochialism, at least that form of parochialism—parochialism with respect to geography—*is* becoming wider, at least in certain respects. The same cannot be said of our temporal parochialism. So the contrast remains.

[4] Someone who finds puzzling the juxtaposition of increasing cosmopolitanism with respect to space and increasing parochialism with respect to time may be thinking (a) that we should be more parochial with respect to both, (b) that we should be less parochial with respect to both, or (c) that either greater parochialism with respect to both or lesser parochialism with respect to both would be more defensible than the juxtaposition of geographical cosmopolitanism with temporal parochialism. Thomas Jefferson would presumably have endorsed the first of these positions. Jefferson opposed the idea of a permanent political constitution and insisted that the dead hand of the past cannot bind the present generation. In arguing for his position, he wrote, in his letter to James Madison of September 6, 1789, that "by the law of nature, one generation is to another as one independent nation to another" (in Julian Boyd, ed., *The Papers of Thomas Jefferson*, Volume 15 [Princeton, NJ: Princeton University Press, 1958], pp. 392–7). In drawing this analogy, Jefferson was insisting on the significance of the distinctions among generations rather than denying the significance of the distinctions among nations.

"presentists" about time whereas our predecessors were "eternalists"; perhaps we believe that only present objects and times exist, whereas they believed that past and future objects and times are equally real. This might help to explain why we have become temporally more parochial even as we have become geographically more cosmopolitan. Of course, such a change in our beliefs would itself require explanation, especially since, in the view of many, it is not a change that is supported by modern science.[5] And one natural suggestion is that, if we are more sympathetic to presentism than were our predecessors, that is because we no longer hold the traditional beliefs that made them feel connected to their ancestors and descendants. But if that is correct, then rather than explaining our growing temporal parochialism, the putative change in our beliefs about the metaphysics of time would instead be explained by it.

Another possible explanation appeals to changes in our understanding of freedom. According to this hypothesis, the kind of freedom we have increasingly come to value in the modern age is the freedom to pursue our present aims and to try to satisfy our present desires. This makes us hostile to claims purportedly made on us by our ancestors and descendants—by the inhabitants of the past and the future—and by traditions we do not now endorse.[6]

---

[5] See, for example, Ted Sider, *Four Dimensionalism* (Oxford: Clarendon Press, 2001), chapter 2.

[6] This is related to the "voluntarist objection" to associative duties, which I have discussed in a number of the essays collected in *Boundaries and Allegiances* (Oxford: Oxford University Press, 2001). See especially chapters 3, 4, and 6. The centrality of the present in modern conceptions of freedom is one of the themes of Jed Rubenfeld's wide-ranging *Freedom and Time* (New Haven, CT: Yale University Press, 2001), which attempts to anchor a theory of constitutional democracy in an alternative account of the temporal dimension of freedom.

But the present-aim conception of freedom, as we might call it, is compatible with the idea that the political institutions that secure our freedom should be global rather than national in scope. Thus, although we have principled reasons for endorsing a form of temporal parochialism, those reasons do not count against geographical cosmopolitanism. Again, of course, there is room to wonder which of the factors cited here is really the explanans and which is the explanandum. Perhaps our growing temporal parochialism explains our attachment to the present-aim conception of freedom, rather than vice versa. Nevertheless, a shift in our understanding of freedom constitutes one possible explanatory factor.

Still another candidate explanation is political. As I have already observed, our increasing geographical cosmopolitanism is not only a moral but also a political and institutional development. People throughout the world share a global politics, an arena of discourse in which arguments are advanced and rebutted, competing interests confront one another, policies are debated, and actors are made aware of the effects of their actions on others and of the likely response of those others. To the extent that we are becoming geographically more cosmopolitan, part of what this means is that the reach of global politics is expanding. It is becoming more comprehensive, more inclusive, and institutionally more sophisticated.[7] Of course, these developments are complex and open to different interpretations. But on any interpretation, there is a clear contrast with the temporal case, because the plain fact is that there is no inter-temporal politics at all, nor could there be. We do not and cannot participate in a shared politics with human beings of other

---

[7] See Joshua Cohen and Charles Sabel, "Extra Rempublicam Nulla Justitia?," *Philosophy & Public Affairs* 34(2006): 147–75.

eras, nor can the generations of the past and the future advocate for their own interests within our politics. This is not to say that one generation cannot influence the political life of subsequent generations. Such influence is pervasive and is the source of the familiar Jeffersonian objection (cited in note 4 above) to allowing the dead hand of the past to constrain those who are now alive. The point is rather that we cannot engage in mutual debate, deliberation, or contestation with generations that do not overlap with ours. In that sense, we cannot share a politics with them. They cannot intervene in our political debates and deliberations except insofar as we choose to speak on their behalf. Moreover, increasing inclusiveness with respect to our own temporal cohort may actually help to produce decreasing inclusiveness with respect to other cohorts, since non-contemporaries must compete with contemporaries for our limited store of time, attention, and resources. If that is correct, then it is not surprising that an increase in geographical cosmopolitanism should be accompanied by an increase in temporal parochialism.

The explanations I have been discussing are neither mutually exclusive nor jointly exhaustive, and I will attempt neither to decide among them nor to canvass other possibilities. In rehearsing a few candidate explanations, moreover, I don't mean to exaggerate either of the contrasting attitudes they purport to explain. On the one hand, our cosmopolitanism, such as it is, is very much a work in progress. It represents one important tendency in contemporary thought and practice, but it has met, and continues to meet, with strong opposition of many different kinds. It is far from clear how politically and culturally robust cosmopolitan attitudes and ideas will prove to be in the long run. For the time being, at least, the power of national and communal identifications and the ferocity of national and communal conflicts make the prospects of cosmopolitanism look uncertain at best.[8] On the other hand—and this is a point of greater direct relevance to the main argument of this book—I think that many people are uneasy about our temporal parochialism. As evidence I would cite, with respect to our attitudes toward the past, the widespread interest in genealogy and the tracing of one's personal ancestry. The extent of this interest suggests that many people have strong desires to establish a sense of connection with their ancestors and to situate themselves in relation to those who lived in earlier times. These are not the desires of people who are indifferent to the past. They are the desires of people who hunger for a history.

With respect to our attitudes toward the future, there are also indications that our temporal parochialism is a source of anxiety. Consider, for example, the large and ever-growing body of apocalyptic and post-apocalyptic literature and film—the rapidly expanding catalogue of novels and movies devoted to stories about the destruction of the Earth; about catastrophic events like plagues, nuclear conflicts, or collisions with heavenly bodies; about the imminent extinction, actual extinction, or near extinction of human life, and about the dystopian aftermath of such events. It does not seem unreasonable to suggest that the imaginative power of these apocalyptic and dystopian fantasies is fueled by a pervasive fear that our planet is in serious trouble, that the fate of our descendants is uncertain, and that the future of our species is by no means assured. These are not the concerns of people to whom

---

[8] These sentences were written before the 2016 Brexit vote in the United Kingdom and the subsequent election of Donald Trump in the United States, both of which served to underscore the intensity of anti-cosmopolitan sentiment in those two countries and beyond.

future generations mean nothing. They are the concerns of people who are fearful about the future of humanity.

I interpret both these sets of phenomena—both the interest in genealogy and ancestry and the popularity of apocalyptic and post-apocalyptic literature and film—as manifestations of uneasiness which serve to confirm the absence of any confident or untroubled or normatively articulate understanding of our place in time or our relations to people living at other times. The same uneasiness helps to explain why it is not uncommon for issues of public policy that implicate our attitudes toward the past or the future—issues ranging from the teaching of history to the protection of the environment—to stir controversy and provoke debate. All these things indicate that our temporal parochialism is only part of the story. It may be true that, as compared with more traditional and more religious societies, we have an evaluatively impoverished understanding of the connections among the generations. Our thinking about those connections is not informed by any very rich or determinate set of values. Yet we are hardly uninterested in our relations to our predecessors and successors, and the very poverty of our evaluative thought about our place in the chain of generations is experienced by many people as a problem. It is experienced as a condition of privation, as an evaluative infirmity that stands in need of a remedy.

I have been speaking about our attitudes both toward our ancestors and toward our descendants. But my primary concern in this book is with our attitudes toward future generations in particular, and so I won't have anything further to say about our attitudes either toward our predecessors or toward the past more generally. Those topics are very rich, but they are topics for another day. Nor will I pursue any further the question of how to explain the contrast between our geographical cosmopolitanism and our temporal parochialism.[9] The question is interesting, but nothing that I want to say here depends on it, and so I will set it aside and will focus exclusively on questions about our attitudes toward future generations.

One urgent matter of public concern that implicates those attitudes is the topic of climate change. The dominant view among those who have seriously considered the question is that climate change poses a grave threat to our planet and to human life in particular. And although experts disagree about exactly how costly it will be for us to take effective action to minimize or mitigate the impact of climate change, by most accounts the costs are likely to be significant.[10] Suppose that that is so. And suppose that failure to take such action will allow processes to unfold that will have drastic and potentially devastating effects on the lives of those who come after us. Some of the effects of climate change are already apparent, and in the absence of concerted action, more dramatic effects will be felt during our lifetimes. But the effects on people who come after us will be more devastating still. And eventually, the Earth may become uninhabitable by humans. Indeed, on the day that I wrote these words, *The New York Times* cited unnamed scientists as saying the Earth could become uninhabitable by the end of this century.[11]

---

[9] For an imaginative exploration, from a very different perspective, of the comparative normative significance of spatial and temporal distance, see Larry Temkin, "Rationality with Respect to People, Places, and Times," *Canadian Journal of Philosophy* 45(2016): 576–608.

[10] John Broome, relying on the work of Duncan Foley and others, argues that the problem could in principle be solved without requiring any net sacrifice from anyone. See Broome, *Climate Matters* (New York: W.W. Norton & Co., 2012), pp. 44–8.

[11] Coral Davenport, "Optimism Faces Grave Realities at Climate Talks," *The New York Times*, December 1, 2014, p. A1.

If that is right, then we are faced with a choice. We must decide what costs we are willing to bear, and how far we are willing to alter our lives, in order to arrest or minimize processes that will otherwise create miserable conditions of life for many future inhabitants of this planet and may lead eventually to human extinction. The precise character of the choice will differ for people in different societies. The most affluent societies have historically been responsible for most of the greenhouse gas emissions that are the primary human cause of climate change, and those of us who live in such societies may have to decide how sharply we are willing to reduce our standard of living. By contrast, those who live in less-developed societies that hope to achieve affluence as great as ours may instead have to decide to what extent they are willing to forgo or delay the gains to which they aspire. But these choices have a common structure. In both affluent and developing societies, decisions must be made about the extent to which those now living are prepared to incur costs and to accept certain forms of hardship so that those who live later don't have to endure much greater hardships, and so that human beings can continue to inhabit the Earth.[12]

Climate change has attracted the attention of researchers in many different disciplines. Philosophers, in particular, have been

---

[12] Many models of the economics of climate change effectively build in the contrast between temporal parochialism and geographical cosmopolitanism discussed above. They incorporate a "pure time preference" that leads to discounting the interests of future generations, but they assign full value to the interests of everyone in the world now living. There is no provision for a "pure space preference." For relevant discussion, see Dale Jamieson, *Reason in a Dark Time* [New York: Oxford University Press, 2014], pp. 125–6. See also Thomas Schelling, "Intergenerational and International Discounting," *Risk Analysis* 20(2000): 833–7.

especially interested in the issues of justice and responsibility that it raises.[13] How does justice require the costs of preventing or mitigating the worst effects of climate change to be shared among the nations of the world, which differ widely in their wealth, population, developmental level, and historical levels of greenhouse gas emissions? To what extent can the problem of climate change be addressed through the existing system of nation-states and international organizations, and to what extent does the need to confront this problem call for the development of new structures of global governance? What would those structures have to look like, in order to satisfy the demands of justice? And what are the responsibilities of individuals to modify their own behavior and to mobilize politically in support of efforts to combat climate change?

These are all important questions. But there are some prior questions that also need to be addressed. Most fundamentally, there is the question of why we should care about climate change at all. In particular, why should we care about those effects of climate change that will not unfold until after we are gone? As I have said, the effects of climate change are already being felt, and, in the absence of concerted action and perhaps even with it, they are likely to become steadily more pronounced throughout the remainder of our lives. Most people would agree that we have reasons to be concerned about any effects of climate change that will have a significant impact on our own lives, and, in practice, it is the severity

---

[13] See, in addition to the important books by Broome and Jamieson cited in notes 10 and 12, respectively, Stephen Gardiner, *A Perfect Moral Storm: The Ethical Tragedy of Climate Change* (New York: Oxford University Press, 2011); Henry Shue, *Climate Justice* (New York: Oxford University Press, 2014); and the many significant articles about climate change by Simon Caney.

of these effects that probably has the best chance of motivating us to do something about the problem. But suppose that, even if climate change were to proceed unchecked, most of us could live out the remainder of our lives without any significant hardship ensuing. If this were true, would we still have reason to be concerned about those effects of climate change that will be felt only after we are gone and will affect only future generations? And, if so, why exactly?

In attempting to answer these questions, I think it is important to take seriously the idea that what we are discussing is the fate of future *generations*. Philosophers sometimes use the phrase "future generations" interchangeably with the phrase "future people," and in some contexts that bit of usage is perfectly innocent. But the word *generations* has distinctive content, and the widespread use of the phrase "future generations" is significant. It testifies to the fact that the people of the future—the people whose existence and flourishing are in question—do not present themselves to us in thought simply as an unstructured group. They present themselves to us as temporally and causally ordered. What is in question is the future of a chronological *succession* of generations, each produced causally, in the familiar way, by the one preceding it. When we ask why we should care about future generations, we are not simply asking why we should care whether people exist in the future or how those people fare. We are asking why we should care that the chronological succession of generations, which has delivered each of us here, should extend into the future under more rather than less favorable conditions. The difference between these questions is important. If we ask why we should care about future people, for example, or what our responsibilities toward them are, we may be tempted to suppose that the only thing that is at issue is the weight we should give to their interests or their welfare. We may fail to consider the possibility that the importance to us of future generations lies partly in the fact that they are our *successors*, that their existence extends the chain of generations in which we ourselves are participants. So just by the way we have framed the question, we may have diverted attention away from an important part of the answer. Yet if that is part of the answer, it is hiding in plain sight, its presence revealed whenever we use the phrase "future generations."

But who exactly is included within the scope of that phrase? On one interpretation, which I will call the *unrestricted* interpretation, future generations include all those people who are not yet alive but will be someday. So they include many people who will be born during our own lifetimes. Indeed, since it has been estimated that 267 people are born throughout the world each minute, it now includes thousands of people who will be born by the time you finish reading this chapter, and who will then no longer fall within the scope of the phrase "future generations."[14] On a second interpretation, which I will call the *restricted* interpretation, the phrase refers only to those people who will not be born until after everyone now living is dead. On this interpretation, the future people who will be born while you are reading the rest of this chapter do not belong, even now, to future generations.

Of course, both interpretations include indexical elements like "now" and "not yet," so on either interpretation the class of future people is constantly changing as the reference of these terms changes. And this reminds us that the idea of a succession of future generations oversimplifies a more complex reality. New generations of human beings do not appear all at once and replace previous generations all at once. Instead, as Brian Barry says, "'Generations' are an abstraction from a continuous process of population

---

[14] See www.nytimes.com/2010/07/30/world/30population.html?_r=0.

replacement."[15] There are really two different points here. The first is that human parents do not in general cease to exist when their children are born, so at any given time the human population includes the members of different generations. The second point is that chains of human generations are constituted ultimately at the level of individuals and their ancestors and descendants, and these chains of individual descent do not follow a uniform timetable. So the lives of different people who are taken to belong to the same generation usually overlap temporally rather than completely coinciding. As I will later emphasize, we should not conclude from these points that the significance of the idea of "future generations" is to be given a purely reductionist understanding. We should not suppose, in other words, that any concern we have for future generations must really be a concern for some particular line of individual descent, such as, for instance, our own. Surprisingly, perhaps, future generations can themselves be objects of concern, despite the respects in which they are "an abstraction." This is just to say that it can matter to us that human beings as a group continue to have descendants, whether or not we as individuals do. But here I am getting ahead of myself. I will return to this point in the next two chapters, where I will offer my own account of the reasons future generations do and should matter to us.

A point of more immediate concern is that the distinction between the restricted and unrestricted interpretations has implications for how we understand the question I have posed. The question of why we should care about the effects of climate change on future generations comes into sharpest focus if we give that

---

[15] Brian Barry, "Justice Between Generations," in P.M.S. Hacker and J. Raz, eds., *Law, Morality and Society: Essays in Honour of H.L.A. Hart* (Oxford: Clarendon Press, 1977), pp. 268–84, at 268.

phrase the restricted rather than the unrestricted interpretation. If we gave it the unrestricted interpretation, then some of the people we would be asking about, in asking why we should care about the effects of climate change on future generations, would be people whom we may eventually meet and with whom we may eventually come to have personal relationships that matter to us. So any adequate answer to the question of why we should care prospectively about the fate of future generations in the unrestricted sense would have to take into account, and would surely be influenced by, the fact that we may eventually establish actual relationships with some individuals who belong to those generations. But what I want to ask is why we should care about the fate of people whom nobody now alive will ever meet, and who will therefore remain forever outside the boundaries of our collective experience? Why should we be prepared to bear any costs at all for the sake of these strangers, whose identities are unknown to us and with whom we will never be acquainted? We will be gone, forever, by the time they arrive on the scene. Why should their fate be a source of concern for us now? Why should we be prepared to compromise the quality of our own lives in any way in order to improve or to avoid worsening the quality of theirs? More radically, why should we be troubled if we learn that, as a predictable result of climate change, the Earth will become completely uninhabitable and the chain of human generations will simply come to an end, once we and everyone whom any of us will ever meet has died? If these are the questions we wish to ask, then we will want to give the phrase *future generations* the restricted rather than the unrestricted interpretation.

We should not suppose that only a moral skeptic would think to raise these questions. For anyone who is tempted to think of morality in broadly relational terms—that is, as a set of values and norms that govern our relationships with one another—it may seem genuinely unclear what morality has to say about the implications of our actions for those people with whom neither we nor anyone else now living will ever have a personal relationship of any kind. Certainly it must have some things to say. On any plausible moral view, for example, it would be wrong to deploy a nuclear bomb that was timed to detonate in a major population center in two hundred years, killing many people who do not yet exist. Yet since, as it seems, nobody who was alive when the bomb was deployed would ever have a personal relationship with any of the prospective victims of the detonation, the basis for this judgment of wrongness in distinctively relational norms may not be immediately apparent. More generally, it remains unclear how much guidance the moral norms that govern our relations to our contemporaries can provide when we are thinking about the implications of our actions for people with whom nobody now alive will ever have a personal relationship. So even when the point of raising the questions I have mentioned is to explore our specifically moral responsibilities with respect to future generations, those questions need not be expressions of general moral skepticism. They may instead reflect genuine puzzlement about the ways in which the reach of morality extends into the future.

At the same time, it should be noted that the questions as I framed them make no reference to morality in particular. They are questions about our reasons for caring what happens to future generations. They do not presuppose that any reasons we may have must be moral reasons, nor is that an assumption we should make in thinking about possible answers to these questions. If we have reasons to care about future generations, those reasons may or may not be found within the realm of morality.

What is true is that any answer to the question of why we should care about the effects of climate change on future generations, or about the threat it poses of eventual human extinction, must draw on ideas of value of the kind I began this chapter by discussing. It must draw on some conception of the value or importance of human continuity and survival. If what I have said is right, most of us have no settled and well-developed conception of this kind. We exhibit a form of temporal parochialism, but we are not secure in our parochialism. To some extent, at least, we seem preoccupied with our place in the chain of generations despite ourselves. And our very ambivalence evidences a tacit recognition that the fate of our successors implicates values that are important to us. Or so it seems to me.

My aim in this book is, in effect, to excavate the sources of our ambivalence. Ultimately, I want to suggest, we have richer evaluative resources than we may realize for thinking about the future of humanity, and we have stronger and more varied reasons than we commonly acknowledge for caring about the fate of our successors. If this is correct, then we gain in self-understanding when we come to appreciate these resources and these reasons. We gain in our understanding of who we are and of the things that really matter to us. There may be practical gains to be had as well. If it is true that we have richer evaluative resources than we realize for thinking about the future of humanity, then these are resources that may be mobilized to address those contemporary conditions, including but not limited to climate change, that pose such serious threats to future generations.

Despite the unsettled state of our evaluative thought about the future, questions about our responsibilities to future generations have been the subject of a large philosophical literature that has grown up over the past several decades. One of the earliest and most important contemporary contributions to that literature was made by John Rawls, whose theory of justice includes a "just savings principle" that governs the distribution of resources among different generations. The just savings principle has some attractive features, but Rawls's discussion of it is relatively brief and undeveloped as compared with other elements of his theory, and his account of the principle's basis changed significantly over time.[16] Much of the subsequent philosophical literature about future generations has developed not in response to Rawls but rather in response to the brilliant and pioneering work of Derek Parfit in Part Four of *Reasons and Persons*.[17] Parfit's work, and much of the literature responding to it, is of broadly utilitarian orientation. One

---

[16] Rawls discusses the just savings principle in Section 44 of the first edition of *A Theory of Justice* (Cambridge, MA: Harvard University Press, 1971). He then modifies his account incrementally in a series of subsequent discussions, including those in Section 44 of the revised edition of *Theory* (Cambridge, MA: Harvard University Press, 1999) and Lecture VII.6 of *Political Liberalism* (New York: Columbia University Press, 1993), and culminating in the discussion in sections 49.2 and 49.3 of *Justice as Fairness: A Restatement* (Cambridge, MA: Harvard University Press, 2001). The primary locus of change is in the account of the motivation for the adoption of the principle by the parties in the "original position." Initially, Rawls said that the parties were to be understood as representatives of family lines whose concern for their descendants extended over at least two generations. Eventually he abandoned this assumption, which required a departure from his default characterization of the parties as mutually disinterested. He proposed instead that the mutually disinterested parties, belonging to a single generation but not knowing which one, would adopt the savings principle that they would want past generations to have followed. He credits this idea to Thomas Nagel and Derek Parfit, and notes that it was independently proposed by Jane English in "Justice Between Generations," *Philosophical Studies* 31(1977): 91–104.

[17] Oxford: Clarendon Press, 1984. Of course, Rawls's work has also attracted significant attention. For an early critical discussion, see Brian Barry, "Justice Between Generations," in Hacker and Raz, eds., *Law, Morality and Society: Essays in Honour of H.L.A. Hart*.

of its primary aims is to formulate a "principle of beneficence" that seems credible when applied to questions about future generations. Beneficence, as Parfit understands it, is the part of morality that is concerned with "human well-being,"[18] and for utilitarians this is the entirety of morality.[19] But Parfit uses the term "principle of beneficence" instead of "principle of utility" to refer to this part of morality. He does this, he says, because although utilitarians think that a principle concerned with well-being comprises the whole of morality, some non-utilitarians accept such a principle as just one element of their wider moral outlook, which may also include, for example, a commitment to individual rights.[20] The term "principle of beneficence," then, is Parfit's label for the principle concerning well-being which, in some version, utilitarians take to comprise the whole of morality and which some non-utilitarians instead take to comprise just one element of morality. An adequate principle of beneficence, it is hoped, would enable us to determine how, when assessing actions and policies that will affect future generations, we should balance considerations about the number of people who will come to exist against considerations about the quality of life that those who come to exist will enjoy. And it would

[18] *Reasons and Persons*, pp. 370, 393.

[19] One caveat: utilitarians frequently understand beneficence to include a concern not solely for human well-being, as Parfit seems to suggest, but for the well-being of all sentient creatures. Except where the context indicates otherwise, I will ignore this complication and rely on Parfit's narrower understanding, but this is simply for ease of exposition and does not affect the substance of my discussion. All the points I want to make about utilitarian and beneficence-based approaches to future generations would remain exactly the same if beneficence were understood to include a concern for the well-being of all sentient creatures.

[20] *Reasons and Persons*, p. 366.

help to resolve puzzles arising from the fact that our actions may affect the identities of those who will come to exist. These questions and puzzles, and others like them, are taken to define the field of "population ethics."

Utilitarian considerations have long played a prominent role in the discussion of our responsibilities to future generations, in part because the basic logic of utilitarianism—with its imperative to maximize the good and its identification of the good with happiness or welfare or well-being—makes questions about the status of future generations as objects of moral concern seem immediately salient. If our concern is to maximize welfare, then the welfare of future people would appear offhand to be just as relevant as the welfare of the living. And in addition to making the questions salient, of course, utilitarianism also proposes answers to them. Each of the most familiar versions of the theory seems to have clear implications for questions about our responsibilities toward future generations.

Up to a point, this reflects one of the great historical strengths of the utilitarian tradition. Because of their single-minded focus on what will enhance welfare or well-being, utilitarians have never been willing to take for granted the moral significance of distinctions that have the effect of restricting the scope of welfarist concern, no matter how morally fundamental those distinctions may previously have been taken to be. They have refused to assume, for instance, that the suffering of non-human animals counts for less than the suffering of humans,[21] or that the suffering of people in distant lands matters less than the suffering of our compatriots, or, similarly, that the welfare of future people counts for less than the

---

[21] This is, of course, a point that is obscured if one thinks of beneficence as concerned solely with *human* well-being.

welfare of our contemporaries. In consequence, utilitarians have been among the first to insist on the importance of questions about the ethical treatment of non-human animals, about the obligations of affluent individuals and societies to help alleviate global poverty, and, in the case of immediate interest to us here, about our responsibilities toward future generations. In raising and pressing such questions, utilitarians have exerted pressure to widen the scope of moral concern. Since utilitarians and non-utilitarians alike regard the tendency toward greater inclusiveness as one of the most important achievements of modern moral thought, the inclusive pressure exerted by utilitarian ideas speaks to non-utilitarians as well. So whatever they think of the utilitarian's answers to questions about the ethical treatment of animals or global poverty or future generations, non-utilitarians rarely deny the significance of the questions.

This points to another factor that also helps to explain the prominence of utilitarian considerations in discussions of future generations. On the whole, and despite some notable exceptions such as Rawls, non-utilitarians have been slower to develop alternative approaches of their own to the topic.[22] In part, this may be because, as Parfit suggests, some non-utilitarians accept a general principle of beneficence as one element of their moral outlook, and because they agree with utilitarians that beneficence is the ultimate source

---

[22] I am counting non-welfarist and non-maximizing forms of consequentialism as belonging to the utilitarian tradition broadly construed, and so when I speak of "non-utilitarian" views I am referring only to views that depart from consequentialism altogether. Non-welfarist and non-maximizing forms of consequentialism may avoid some (though not all) of the doubts that I express in the text about more familiar forms of utilitarianism. However, although I cannot argue the point here, I believe that they are subject to similar doubts that are at least as severe.

of our responsibilities to future generations. But it is also because most non-utilitarian outlooks lack the kind of simple structure that, in theory at least, allows utilitarianism to be applied straightforwardly to virtually any first-order moral question. And insofar as non-utilitarian outlooks include elements other than a principle of beneficence, the possible bearing of those other elements on questions about our responsibilities to future generations is often far from transparent.[23]

Yet despite the prominence of utilitarian ideas in the literature on future generations, my own approach to the subject will not be utilitarian. I will not pursue the quest for a principle of beneficence that can guide our conduct with respect to future generations, nor will I frame my discussion with reference to the questions of population ethics. One reason for this is evident from what I said at the beginning of this chapter. I am interested in the broad topic of how future generations feature in or are related to our practical and evaluative thought as a whole. I am concerned with questions about what hopes we may have for our successors, about whether and why their survival and flourishing matter to us, and about what reasons we may have for concerning ourselves with their fates. From this perspective, questions about our moral duties or obligations toward them—whether we conceive of such duties in utilitarian or non-utilitarian terms—constitute only a subset of the questions that are worth considering. Values of many different kinds may have roles to play in our reflections about future

---

[23] For an attempt to apply the relational apparatus of Scanlonian contractualism to such questions, see Rahul Kumar, "Wronging Future People: A Contractualist Proposal," in A. Gosseries and L. Meyer, eds., *Intergenerational Justice* (Oxford: Oxford University Press, 2009), pp. 251–72. This paper draws on Kumar's earlier "Who Can Be Wronged?," *Philosophy & Public Affairs* 31(2003): 99–118.

generations, and they need not all take the form of moral obligations. Moreover, there are costs to a narrow and highly moralized focus on questions of duty and obligation. Such a focus may discourage us from thinking broadly about the kinds of meaning and value that we attach to the continuation of human life on Earth. It may tempt us to suppose, wrongly in my opinion, that future generations matter to us only insofar as they add to our already abundant stock of potentially burdensome obligations. In so doing, it may contribute to the well-known problem of obligation fatigue, while blinding us to some of the most important ways in which our values orient us toward the future, or would do if we paid attention to them.

Even within the territory of moral duty or obligation, an exclusive emphasis on beneficence-based duties seems to me a mistake. As I said a moment ago, it is a strength of utilitarianism that, by virtue of its single-minded emphasis on maximizing welfare or well-being, it exerts pressure to widen the scope of moral concern to include groups that have often been excluded: non-human animals, distant strangers, future people. Yet its strength is also its weakness. The same focus on maximizing welfare that leads utilitarians to raise important questions about the ethical treatment of previously excluded groups also leads them, at times, to give very implausible answers to those questions. So, for example, although the most familiar versions of the principle of utility appear to have clear implications for questions of population ethics, those implications strike most people as being manifestly unacceptable. Consider, for example, the "total" version of utilitarianism, which directs us to maximize the total aggregate welfare of all human beings. This seems to entail that we are morally required to keep increasing the size of the human population so long as each new person added yields a net increase in the total aggregate welfare of humanity, even if the average level of welfare per person falls significantly.[24] Or consider instead "average" utilitarianism, which directs us to maximize average rather than total welfare. According to this version of the view, the size of the population doesn't matter in itself so long as it comprises the people who, on average, enjoy the highest attainable levels of well-being. In some circumstances, the imperative might be to cultivate and maintain a relatively small population of people to whom happiness comes easily and who are robustly disposed to contentment. Neither of these positions strikes most people as being at all credible.[25,26]

---

[24] Henry Sidgwick articulates this feature of total utilitarianism with his customary clarity, and distinguishes it from the implications of average utilitarianism, in *The Methods of Ethics*, 7th edition (Macmillan & Co., 1907; republished by Hackett Publishing Company [Indianapolis, 1981]), pp. 415–16.

[25] Wayne Sumner makes the point forcefully—perhaps a bit too forcefully—when discussing the implications of the average view. He says, "it seems likely that the optimum population defined by the average theory would be very small indeed, as compared with our current level, and that the theory would not be squeamish about the means to be used in achieving that optimum" ("Classical Utilitarianism and the Population Optimum," in R. I. Sikora and B. Barry, eds., *Obligations to Future Generations* [Philadelphia, PA: Temple University Press, 1978], pp. 91–111, at 105–6).

[26] In a series of influential papers about population issues published in the 1960s and 1970s, Jan Narveson argued that both positions rest on implausible interpretations of utilitarianism. In Narveson's view, the most defensible version of utilitarianism holds (roughly) that we should maximize not total or average welfare or happiness as such but rather the total happiness of everyone who is affected by our actions. He maintains that a utilitarianism of this kind can avoid the implausible implications of both the total and average views with respect to questions of population. (See Narveson, "Utilitarianism and New Generations,"

Parfit himself insists on the implausibility of the answers given by both the total and the average versions of utilitarianism, and most of the beneficence-based literature is preoccupied with trying to resolve the puzzles that arise when one seeks to formulate a credible alternative to the total and average views. The aim is to find a principle of beneficence that does not have what are acknowledged to be "absurd" or "repugnant" or "ridiculous" or otherwise unacceptable implications when applied to questions of population ethics. Yet despite the fact that the quest for a suitable principle of beneficence has for decades featured prominently in the philosophical literature dealing with our responsibilities toward future generations, no plausible principle of this kind has yet been identified.[27]

How one interprets the significance of this fact will depend on one's wider moral outlook. For utilitarians, beneficence is the whole of morality, and so for them an adequate principle of beneficence

---

Mind 76[1967]: 62–72; "Moral Problems of Population," *The Monist* 57[1973]: 62–86; and "Future People and Us," in Sikora and Barry, eds., *Obligations to Future Generations*, pp. 38–60.) In *Reasons and Persons*, however, Parfit argues at length that "person-affecting" forms of utilitarianism cannot avoid such implications. Nevertheless, the question of whether some version of a "person-affecting restriction" can help to solve the puzzles of population ethics remains the subject of controversy. For discussion, see, for example, Gustaf Arrhenius, "Can the Person-Affecting Restriction Solve the Problems in Population Ethics?," in Roberts and Wasserman, eds., *Harming Future Persons* (Dordrecht: Springer Verlag, 2009), pp. 289–314, and M. A. Roberts, "Population Axiology," in Hirose and Olson, eds., *The Oxford Handbook of Value Theory* (New York: Oxford University Press, 2015), pp. 399–423.

[27] Toward the end of his life Parfit believed he was making progress toward such a principle. The last paper he published on the subject before his death was "Can We Avoid the Repugnant Conclusion?," *Theoria* 82(2016): 110–17.

would give a complete answer to the question of what responsibilities we have toward future generations. And without an adequate principle of beneficence, not only are our responsibilities toward future generations left uncertain but the entire content of morality is called into question. This makes the quest for such a principle—for what Parfit calls *Theory X*—a matter of the utmost importance. But for non-utilitarians, beneficence is at most one aspect of morality, and it is not clear that we need, even as one element of morality among others, an extremely general principle of beneficence of the kind that utilitarians want: a principle modeled on the principles of total and average utility but modified to avoid their unwelcome implications. Nor is it clear to non-utilitarians that we should expect all of the questions of population ethics to have answers. Parfit says that Theory X "would have acceptable implications when applied to all of the choices that we ever make, including those that affect both the identities and the number of future people." Indeed, he also says that "[i]n a complete moral theory, we cannot avoid the question of how many people there should ever be,"[28] and this is not, in itself, a question about any of our choices at all. Yet non-utilitarians may not share the conceptions of moral theory and of completeness that make this last question seem unavoidable, and some of them may not even be confident that they understand the question. Nor are non-utilitarians bound to agree that we should expect to find a principle of beneficence that will have acceptable implications when applied to all the choices human beings ever make.

The idea that non-utilitarians can make do without a general principle of beneficence may seem plainly mistaken. As I have noted, Parfit says that many people accept a theory that includes

[28] *Reasons and Persons*, p. 405.

both a general principle of beneficence and a set of rights that are taken to constrain beneficence,[29] and it may seem that any minimally credible non-utilitarian outlook must include such a principle. After all, ideas of beneficence, and related ideas of charity, liberality, and humanity, have a long history in moral thought, much longer than the history of utilitarianism itself. Moreover, non-utilitarians have reasons of their own for distinguishing between justice and beneficence, and for treating each of them as defining an important part of the content of morality. However, beneficence and related ideas have historically been understood in many different ways, as has the distinction between beneficence and justice.[30] In our day, non-utilitarians frequently acknowledge duties of humanitarianism that are sometimes taken to fall under the heading of beneficence rather than justice, but these duties are typically treated as defining a kind of moral minimum. They spell out our responsibilities to assist strangers in emergencies or in circumstances of extreme deprivation or suffering. When utilitarians speak of a "principle of beneficence," by contrast, they have in mind a kind of generalized imperative to do good, a principle modeled on the principles of total and average utility themselves. And although there are some non-utilitarians who accept, as one element of their view among others, a principle of beneficence so understood, others do not.

[29] *Reasons and Persons*, p. 366.

[30] As Charles Beitz has recently observed, for example, Cicero thought that our duties of beneficence toward people with whom we have no special relationship are quite limited. They include such things as giving advice and letting someone else light his fire from yours (Charles Beitz, "Cicero on Justice and Beneficence," unpublished draft of August 17, 2015, p. 9). For critical discussion of Cicero's position, see Martha Nussbaum, "Duties of Justice, Duties of Material Aid: Cicero's Problematic Legacy," *Journal of Political Philosophy* 8(2000): 176–206.

It will be helpful to have some terminology to mark the distinction between non-utilitarians of these two types. I will refer to non-utilitarians who accept, as one element of their outlook among others, a utilitarian-style principle of beneficence, as *inclusive* non-utilitarians.[31] And I will refer to those who do not accept such a principle as *exclusive* non-utilitarians. For ease of reference, I will say that inclusive non-utilitarians accept a "utilitarian conception of beneficence" and that exclusive non-utilitarians do not. As I have noted, many exclusive non-utilitarians have their own ideas of beneficence, and I will refer to these as "non-utilitarian conceptions of beneficence." Although these non-utilitarian conceptions differ from one another in various respects, none of them conceptualizes beneficence as a kind of general imperative to do good.

It does not follow from what has been said that considerations of beneficence have no role to play in the thinking of exclusive non-utilitarians about future generations.[32] Nor does it follow that these exclusivists are immune to the puzzles and paradoxes that have bedeviled the quest for a utilitarian-style "principle of beneficence." But it is at least an open question whether beneficence as interpreted by exclusive non-utilitarians does give rise to those puzzles and paradoxes. To an extent that cannot be determined in the absence of careful investigation, the source of the puzzles may instead lie in

---

[31] A good example might be W.D. Ross, whose initial summary of his pluralist deontology includes beneficence as one of several independent *prima facie* duties. See Ross, *The Right and the Good* (Oxford: Clarendon Press, 1930; rev. ed. 2002 [ed. Philip Stratton-Lake]), p. 21. For reasons that need not detain us here, Ross goes on to explain that, ultimately, he regards the duty of beneficence not as equivalent to but as an instance of a slightly more general duty to "produce as much good as possible" (p. 27).

[32] In Chapter Four, I will suggest a role that non-utilitarian considerations of beneficence do have.

assumptions about the nature of beneficence that only utilitarians (and inclusive non-utilitarians) make or in the very general and context-independent character of the principle of beneficence that they seek.[33] And even if this is not so—even if non-utilitarian conceptions of beneficence are just as subject as utilitarian conceptions to the puzzles of population ethics—the fact that non-utilitarians, whether inclusive or exclusive, also recognize moral ideas other than beneficence means they have independent moral resources whose significance for questions about future generations is worth exploring. From a non-utilitarian perspective, therefore, a single-minded emphasis on beneficence-based duties, even within the context of specifically moral reflection about the future, would be a mistake.[34]

---

[33] In her 1983 Presidential Address to the Pacific Division of the American Philosophical Association (reprinted with revisions as "Utilitarianism and the Virtues," *Mind* 94[1985]: 196–209), Philippa Foot made a suggestion of this kind about the source of the so-called "paradox of deontology." In an article replying to Foot ("Agent-Centered Restrictions, Rationality, and the Virtues," *Mind* 94[1985]: 409–19), I tried to show that her specific arguments, which appealed to the content of the virtue of benevolence, were unsuccessful, at least as applied to puzzles about the rationale for deontological restrictions. Nevertheless, I am tempted by the thought that a version of her general strategy may appropriately be applied to some of the puzzles of population ethics.

Judith Thomson suggests an even more radical critique of the utilitarian conception of beneficence when she argues that "there is no such thing as goodness." See Thomson, "The Right and the Good," *Journal of Philosophy* 94(1997): 273–98, and Thomson, *Goodness and Advice*, ed. Amy Gutmann (Princeton, NJ: Princeton University Press, 2001), where the quoted phrase appears at p. 41.

[34] For related remarks about the perils of an overemphasis on beneficence, see James Woodward, "The Non-Identity Problem," *Ethics* 96(1986): 804–31, at pp. 807–8.

I have been explaining why I do not plan to frame my discussion of future generations in utilitarian or beneficence-based terms. The tendency of such a framing is to narrow the focus of reflection to questions of moral duty and responsibility, whereas I am interested in the broader topic of how future generations feature in or are related to our practical and evaluative thought as a whole. And even where moral duty and responsibility are concerned, I believe it is a mistake to concentrate exclusively or primarily on beneficence-based duties. As applied to questions of population, the quest for a "principle of beneficence" of the kind favored by utilitarians and inclusive non-utilitarians has to date been notable primarily for the depth and intractability of the puzzles it has uncovered. Yet exclusive non-utilitarians do not accept the need for such a principle, and both inclusive and exclusive non-utilitarians have other moral ideas whose relevance for questions about future generations should not be overlooked. So insofar as we wish to engage in moral reflection about the future, we should not limit our reflections to the questions of population ethics nor should we think about the issues solely in beneficence-based terms.

There is another reason to avoid framing questions about future generations with reference to a utilitarian conception of beneficence, for such an approach is limiting in a way that goes beyond those already noted. It asks how we should take the well-being of future people into account in our decisions and actions, and it attempts to answer that question by identifying a suitable principle of beneficence to guide us. It thereby frames the issues from the outset as ones pertaining exclusively to the welfare or well-being of future generations. This neglects the point I made earlier about the significance of the word "generations." It neglects the possibility that part of what is important to us about future generations is precisely the fact that they are *generations*: that they are participants, as we are, in the same chain of human succession.[35] As I will explain more fully in the chapters to follow, I believe that this point is significant—whether its significance is understood in moral or in non-moral terms—and that it is a mistake to overlook it.

Finally, there is a practical difficulty with a purely utilitarian approach, at least insofar as one thinks it would be desirable for people to take more seriously problems like climate change and nuclear proliferation, which pose such grave threats to the lives and circumstances of our descendants. From a utilitarian perspective, the ethical significance of future generations lies—roughly speaking—in their status as potential victims or beneficiaries of what we do. But unlike other potential victims and beneficiaries, future generations

---

[35] Roger Scruton makes a similar objection to utilitarianism: "Utilitarianism overlooks the fundamental fact about our concern for future generations, which is that we are concerned for them as *ours*. There is a line of obligation that connects us to those who gave us what we have; and our concern for the future is an extension of that line." (*How to Think Seriously about the Planet: The Case for Environmental Conservatism* [New York: Oxford University Press, 2012], p. 216). And Jonathan Bennett, who describes himself as being "passionately in favour of mankind's having a long future," contrasts a utilitarian approach with his own "strong, personal, unprincipled preference" for the continuation of human life. He adds by way of explanation that he just thinks "it would be a great shame—a pity, *too bad*—if this great biological and spiritual adventure didn't continue." His "pro-humanity stand," he says, "is not a stand in favour of there being animals which answer to this or that general biological or psychological description, but rather a stand in favour of there continuing to be animals descended from members of *my* species, or descended from some of *these* (and here I gesture towards all my human contemporaries)." See Jonathan Bennett, "On Maximizing Happiness," in Sikora and Barry, eds., *Obligations to Future Generations*, pp. 61–73, at 66–7. For additional relevant discussion, see James Lenman, "On Becoming Extinct," *Pacific Philosophical Quarterly* 83(2002): 253–69.

don't actually exist yet. And this obvious fact poses a serious difficulty from a utilitarian perspective, because many utilitarians appeal to sympathy as the primary motive that is supposed to lead people to comply with utilitarian norms. If we ask how a person might come to be stably motivated to maximize the welfare of all human beings, the most common answer within the utilitarian tradition appeals to our capacity for sympathetic identification with others. Many non-utilitarians are skeptical about whether sympathy is, in general, a sufficiently robust and reliable feature of human psychology to provide a secure basis for moral motivation. Whether or not one shares those general doubts, however, all sides are agreed that motives like sympathy are most effective in motivating action when we are confronted in a vivid and immediate way with the plight of people who are suffering. In the aftermath of a natural disaster, for example, televised images of people suffering often elicit an outpouring of assistance, whereas more abstract descriptions of human need generate less of a response. But vividness and immediacy are precisely what are lacking when we contemplate the lives of future generations.[36] So whatever one thinks of the motivational credentials of utilitarianism in general, there are specific reasons for pessimism about the capacity of utilitarian reasoning to motivate strong action in behalf of our descendants.

This point is especially significant in view of the fact, mentioned earlier, that there is no possibility of a genuinely inter-temporal politics in which future generations can represent themselves and defend their own interests. Despite this, any concerted effort to address the problems that threaten future generations will require a

---

[36] This point is also emphasized by Dieter Birnbacher, although he draws different conclusions from it. See Birnbacher, "What Motivates Us to Care for the (Distant) Future?," in Gosseries and Meyer, eds., *Intergenerational Justice*, pp. 273–300, at 282.

politics of some kind, and there is a real question whether the motives that might drive such a politics exist and are sufficiently prevalent and powerful among the living to be efficacious. If such a politics can rely on no motive more powerful than sympathy sustained by the hortatory force of utilitarian moral argument, then I think its prospects are bleak. This gives us practical as well as theoretical reasons for not wanting to restrict ourselves to utilitarian ideas. In saying this, I do not mean to be offering a utilitarian argument for encouraging non-utilitarian motives. My point is rather that, in light of the doubts I have been rehearsing about the motivational efficacy of sympathy, we have additional reasons for not wanting to limit ourselves in advance to a utilitarian approach to problems of future generations. If we find alternative approaches that are intellectually more compelling, they may also prove to be practically more effective.

I began this chapter by contrasting our increasing temporal parochialism with our increasing geographical cosmopolitanism, and by noting that our temporal parochialism is a source of uneasiness. Given this uneasiness, one apparent advantage of utilitarianism is that it treats spatial and temporal distance in the same way. The utilitarian principle provides a unified standard that is meant to govern our treatment of people both in other places and at other times. If, for the reasons I have given, we do not endorse the utilitarian approach, one obvious alternative is to look for a non-utilitarian principle of justice that may provide some other unified standard of the same kind. Perhaps, for example, we can settle on some version of a currently popular philosophical theory like luck-egalitarianism or Rawls's difference principle to fix the content of justice both globally and inter-temporally. But I will not take this approach either.

There are at least three different reasons for this. First, such an approach would narrow and moralize the discussion of future generations in the same way that the beneficence-based literature does, and the considerations that count against narrowing our reflection in this way apply with equal force to the search for non-utilitarian principles of inter-temporal justice. Second, in calling attention to the growing asymmetry in our evaluative attitudes toward spatial and temporal distance, I was describing a feature not of philosophical theories of justice but rather of the evaluative thought of our culture more generally. Even if a philosophical theory treats space and time symmetrically, it cannot eliminate this broader cultural tendency by fiat, and it is the broader tendency that I want to explore. Third, in highlighting the growing asymmetry in our attitudes, I did not mean to suggest that complete symmetry is to be expected, only that these divergent trends call for some explanation, and that, whatever the explanation may be, the form of temporal parochialism that many of us exhibit reflects a certain impoverishment in our evaluative thought about generations past and the future.

In this book, I want to investigate the limits of our parochialism and to consider whether there may be, implicit in our evaluative thought, ideas that bear, in insufficiently recognized ways, on our reasons for concerning ourselves with the fate of future generations. If so, then perhaps those ideas may eventually help us to identify compelling principles of justice that apply to the intergenerational case. Whether the principles in question would apply equally to the case of global justice cannot be known in advance. In the meantime, however, my goal will not be to develop a non-utilitarian principle of inter-temporal distributive justice, but rather to explore some of the pertinent evaluative commitments that I believe to be latent in our existing attitudes. I hope that the investigation of these commitments will help to enrich our understanding of the significance that future generations have for us. This means that my aim in this book is neither to refute temporal parochialism considered as a philosophical theory nor to defend a form of "temporal cosmopolitanism." It is instead to reveal the complexity that is latent in our temporal attitudes despite their overt parochialism.

To anticipate the argument of the next two chapters, I don't think it's true that future generations are nothing more to us than potential beneficiaries or victims of our actions. Even if we no longer accept the traditional narratives that once underwrote people's sense of the continuity among the generations, we remain more invested in the fate of our descendants, and they remain more thoroughly implicated in the structures of value that we rely on in our own lives, than we normally recognize. If that is right, then we may have richer evaluative resources available for thinking about their significance for us than we normally realize. In the next two chapters, I will develop this suggestion further. I will not investigate the nature or extent of any reasons of beneficence we may have for concerning ourselves with the fate of our successors.[37] Instead, I will argue that, quite apart from considerations of beneficence, we have reasons of at least four different kinds for trying to ensure the survival and flourishing of those who come after us: reasons of love, reasons of interest, reasons of valuation, and reasons of reciprocity. Of course, my arguments, even if successful, will not provide us with a fully articulated conception of the values that inform our relations to future generations. But by enriching our understanding of the variety of reasons we already have for caring about their

---

[37] I will return to questions about reasons of beneficence in Chapter Four.

existence and what happens to them, I hope that these arguments will lay the groundwork for further reflection about how we may sensibly conduct ourselves when the fate of our successors is at stake. Even the question of whether there can be a politics of future generations may look different, and may merit additional reflection, once a more complete picture of the normative and motivational resources available to such a politics is in hand.[38]

---

[38] It should be evident that my position is opposed not only to an exclusively beneficence-based account of our reasons for seeking to ensure the survival of humanity but also to the view, which some people have defended, that we should *welcome* the prospect of human extinction. David Benatar, for example, argues that it would be better if human beings became extinct, and that "the concern that humans will not exist at some future time is either a symptom of the human arrogance that our presence makes the world a better place or is some misplaced sentimentalism" (David Benatar, *Better Never to Have Been* [Oxford: Clarendon Press, 2006]). If I am right about the reasons we have to ensure the survival and flourishing of our successors, then Benatar's diagnosis of our concern about human survival is mistaken.

CHAPTER TWO

Reasons to Worry: Interest and Love

Why should we care what happens to people who won't be born until after all of us are long gone? Why should we care whether there *are* any people who are born after we are long gone? Should the prospect of human extinction by the end of this century or the next one trouble us, and if so, why? There is an answer to these questions that is implicit in much of the contemporary philosophical literature dealing with our responsibilities to future generations. The answer is that we have reasons of beneficence to care about the existence of future generations and about the quality of life they will enjoy. However, I am not persuaded that considerations of beneficence, as they are commonly understood in that literature, have either as much normative authority or as much motivational force as many writers appear to believe.

In this chapter and Chapter Three, I will suggest that, quite apart from considerations of beneficence, we have reasons of at least four different kinds to try to ensure the survival and flourishing of those who come after us. When I say that we have reasons of these kinds, I do not mean that everyone does, only that many people do. My aim is not to establish that all rational agents must recognize these reasons. For my purposes, the fact that many people have these reasons is sufficient. At a practical level, it expands the collective repertoire of reasons that may be drawn upon when trying to motivate action aimed at ensuring the survival and flourishing of our successors. And at a theoretical level, it enriches our understanding of the evaluative resources available to us as we contemplate the significance for us of life in the future, after we are gone.

In developing my suggestion, I will build on some of the ideas I discussed in my book *Death and the Afterlife*. The central theme of that book is that our capacity to find value in our activities here and now is more dependent than we realize on the implicit assumption that human life will continue long after we ourselves have died.[1] Many of the activities that we now find it worthwhile to engage in would lose much of their point, and would seem to us much less valuable, if we thought that human life was about to come to an end. Indeed, my conjecture is that the prospect of humanity's imminent extinction would be viewed by many people as catastrophic, even if it would be accomplished in a way that did not reduce the lifespan of anyone who was already alive.

In order to illustrate these ideas, I described a scenario derived from P.D. James's novel *The Children of Men*,[2] in which the human race as a whole has become infertile for unknown reasons. No birth

---

[1] This idea, in one form or another, has no doubt been defended by other philosophers as well. For example, Cheryl Misak says that it constitutes "a fundamental insight of" the pragmatist tradition (see Misak, *Cambridge Pragmatism: From Peirce and James to Ramsey and Wittgenstein* [Oxford: Oxford University Press, 2016], p. 45). Allen Wood argues that the same idea can be found in the work of Fichte (see Wood, *Fichte's Ethical Thought* [Oxford: Oxford University Press, 2016]). Other people have suggested to me that there are related themes in the writings of Heidegger and Levinas. I have not attempted to identify or survey all the historical antecedents of the idea.

[2] London: Faber and Faber, 1992.

has occurred in over twenty-five years, and the extinction of the human race is imminent as an aging population gradually but steadily fades away. It is no part of this scenario that any living person has to die prematurely.³ Instead, human beings are simply fading from the scene: week by week, month by month, year by year.⁴ How would we react if we found ourselves living under these conditions? My conjecture, which I hope people who think carefully about the question will find plausible, is that most of us would find the prospect of humanity's imminent extinction unbearably depressing. Faced with this impending catastrophe, our lives would be suffused with grief and gloom. And the effects on us would extend beyond the realm of the emotions; the point is not just that we would feel

---

³ This is a feature of James's plot that distinguishes it from the plots of many other novels and films about the imminent extinction of humanity, such as Ben H. Winters's *The Last Policeman* trilogy and Lars von Trier's *Melancholia*. In each of those two works, human life is expected to come to an end when a heavenly body (an asteroid in the first case and a "rogue planet" in the second) collides with the Earth, and people's attitudes toward the impending catastrophe are colored by their expectation that they and everyone they love will be killed as part of humanity's destruction. Similarly, the idea that the extinction of humanity might be accomplished without a single individual dying prematurely is at odds with the basic premise of post-apocalyptic novels such as Nevil Shute's Cold War classic *On the Beach* or Cormac McCarthy's harrowing *The Road* (New York: Vintage Books, 2006).

⁴ James's scenario was anticipated by Jonathan Schell, who wrote, in his 1982 book *The Fate of the Earth* (New York: Alfred A. Knopf): "suppose that a substance was released into the environment which had the effect of sterilizing all the people in the world but otherwise leaving them unharmed. Then, as the existing population died off, the world would empty of people, until no one was left. Not one life would have been shortened by a single day, but the species would die" (p. 115).

sad or unhappy or sorrowful. At least as significant is the fact that many of the activities that we had previously regarded as worthwhile would no longer seem to us as appealing. We would see less reason to engage in them. Some of those activities might even seem completely pointless. We might see no reason at all to engage in them. To be sure, some activities, such as spending time with family and friends, would almost certainly continue to seem worthwhile to most people. Overall, however, our capacity to find value in our activities would be seriously eroded.[5]

If, as I believe, this is how many of us would react to the prospect of humanity's imminent extinction, then what are we to make of this reaction? On one interpretation, it would involve a kind of evaluative mistake, for our activities would not really diminish in value if humanity were about to disappear. If it seemed to us otherwise, that would mean only that our grief and depression were blinding us to the continuing value of our pursuits. Even if this were so, of course, the mere fact that we would react this way tells us something striking about the content of our evaluative attachments. It tells us that we have a powerful direct concern for the survival of humanity, so much so that the prospect of humanity's imminent extinction would induce in us a degree of grief and depression strong enough to compromise our ability to lead fulfilling lives. This fact is all the more striking because even the recognition of our personal mortality does not normally have this effect.

But I am tempted by a different interpretation. Far from involving an evaluative mistake, our anticipated reaction to humanity's

---

[5] Schell suggests something similar in Chapter II of *The Fate of the Earth*, especially pp. 154–78, when explaining why the prospect of human extinction resulting from a nuclear holocaust is something that those now living should find appalling.

imminent extinction may instead teach us something unexpected. It may teach us that the actual value of many of our activities depends, to a degree that we do not always recognize or acknowledge, on the survival of humanity long after we ourselves are gone.[6]

Is this really plausible? Which of the activities that we now regard as valuable might actually diminish in value, or lose their value altogether, if the disappearance of humanity were imminent? Perhaps the most straightforward examples are provided by collaborative activities with a long-term, goal-oriented structure, such as activities aimed at finding a cure for cancer, enhancing the seismic safety of bridges, or improving the quality of early childhood education. When individuals engage in such activities, they are contributing to a long-term project, involving the participation of many people over an extended period of time, which, if successful, will eventually provide significant benefits to a large number of people. This is the feature of these activities that makes them

---

[6] A similar conclusion is suggested in the following passage from Cormac McCarthy's *The Road*, p. 187: "His dreams brightened. The vanished world returned. Kin long dead washed up and cast fey sidewise looks upon him. None spoke. He thought of his life. So long ago. A gray day in a foreign city where he stood in a window and watched the street below. Behind him on a wooden table a small lamp burned. On the table books and papers. It had begun to rain and a cat at the corner turned and crossed the sidewalk and sat beneath the cafe awning. There was a woman at a table there with her head in her hands. Years later he'd stood in the charred ruins of a library where blackened books lay in pools of water. Shelves tipped over. Some rage at the lies arranged in their thousands row on row. He picked up one of the books and thumbed through the heavy bloated pages. He'd not have thought the value of the smallest thing predicated on a world to come. It surprised him. That the space which these things occupied was itself an expectation. He let the book fall and took a last look around and made his way out into the cold gray light."

valuable. But it is also a feature that would make them vulnerable to a loss of value if the destruction of humanity were imminent, for if the destruction of humanity were imminent, there would be no chance that the long-term projects would succeed in delivering their intended benefits. What, then, would be the point of engaging in activities like cancer research that are meant to contribute to those projects?

Even if this is granted, however, two further questions suggest themselves. First, it is reasonable to wonder how many of the activities that we regard as valuable actually have this feature. In other words, how many of the valuable activities that people engage in really do have a long-term, goal-oriented structure of the relevant kind? That is the first question. In addition, it is reasonable to wonder whether there are other good-making features, apart from possession of a long-term, goal-oriented structure, that would also be compromised by humanity's imminent extinction and, if so, how many valuable activities have those features? That is the second question.[7]

---

[7] In an unpublished paper ("Value, Trauma, and the Future of Humanity"), R. Jay Wallace presses both of these questions. He agrees that humanity's imminent extinction would erode the actual value of some of our activities, such as those that are structured around a long-term goal that is unlikely to be achieved within our own lifetimes. This may be the case, he suggests, with respect to some medical and scientific research projects and some technology and infrastructure improvement projects. But Wallace believes that, for the most part, our hypothesized reaction to the infertility scenario is best thought of as a traumatized but evaluatively mistaken response to a perceived disaster. There are many valuable activities in which we might have less of a tendency or capacity to engage, because of our traumatized condition, but which would remain just as valuable. This is especially true of activities that fall within what he calls the "intermediate" category (because their value is neither purely experiential nor based on their contribution to any long-term goal). With

It would be a mistake to underestimate the number of activities people engage in whose value derives at least in part from their role in contributing to a worthy long-term goal. True, few of us are cancer researchers. But to arrive at an accurate assessment of the prevalence of goal-oriented activities of the relevant kind, we must also take into account the many other types of research that are aimed at some form of improvement in the human condition, including not only medical research of most kinds but also a great deal of non-medical research in science, engineering, technology, and the social sciences. My examples of seismic safety research and research aimed at improving the quality of early childhood education were meant to illustrate this point. It seems fair to say that the broad category of *meliorative research* adds up to a very sizable human enterprise. And the activities whose value derives from the meliorative aims of such research are not limited to the research

---

respect to many such activities, Wallace says he cannot think of any specific good-making features they possess that would be compromised by humanity's imminent extinction.

Since I agree that some activities would retain some or all of their value even if human life were about to end, and since Wallace agrees that some activities would lose their value, the difference between us is more a matter of emphasis and degree than a deep principled divide. This difference of emphasis and degree reflects an underlying disagreement about how many of our valuable activities have at least some good-making features that would be compromised by humanity's imminent extinction. In part, the source of this disagreement lies in our differing assessments of how many valuable activities have the kind of long-term, goal-oriented structure which, Wallace concedes, does render them liable to have their value undermined by the prospect of human extinction. In part, it lies in our differing assessments of the good-making features of various activities in Wallace's "intermediate" category. I provide my own assessments in the text below.

activities themselves, for the efforts of the researchers and innovators must be supported and supplemented by the efforts of many additional people whose work involves, and derives much of its value from the fact that it involves, building and sustaining the institutions that make that research possible.

Even this understates the case, however, because the focus on research is misleadingly narrow. People do not pursue long-term meliorative aims solely by seeking to acquire additional knowledge. Instead, many meliorative activities are more directly practical. They involve, for example, social and political activism aimed at making the world better or safer or freer or more just. And many programs of social, political, or institutional reform are understood to be long-term projects. Like cancer research, they involve the participation of many different people over a long period of time, and it is understood that their ultimate payoff may not occur until long after the deaths of many of the individual participants.[8] These projects include large-scale efforts to improve the justice of basic social institutions. They also include more localized efforts to improve a particular institution or practice. To the extent that these social and political projects, whether on a global or a social or a local scale, are long-term, collaborative efforts aimed at producing eventual change, they too are vulnerable to a loss of value in the

---

[8] Recall the famous words of Martin Luther King Jr., in a speech delivered in Memphis, Tennessee on April 3, 1968, the day before his assassination: "Like anybody, I would like to live a long life. Longevity has its place. But I'm not concerned about that now. I just want to do God's will. And He's allowed me to go up to the mountain. And I've looked over. And I've seen the Promised Land. I may not get there with you. But I want you to know tonight, that we, as a people, will get to the promised land!" (full text available online at www.americanrhetoric.com/speeches/mlkivebeentothemountaintop.htm).

face of human extinction. The point of trying to make our social world a better place in the long run is bound to be compromised if that world is going to disappear in the short run.

This brings us to the second question: the question of whether there are additional good-making features, apart from possession of a long-term, goal-oriented structure, that would also be compromised by humanity's imminent extinction, and, if so, how many valuable activities have those features? I believe that there are a number of these additional good-making features, and that a significant number of valuable activities have at least some of them. Let me mention three features that are especially noteworthy.

First, many individual activities have among their implicit good-making features the specific feature of belonging to an ongoing practice or process that is itself valuable. To see why this is a good-making feature, let me approach the question indirectly, by asking what people mean when they say, as they often do, that they want to be part of something larger than themselves. Such remarks are suggestive, and it seems clear that many people attach special value to activities that they regard as capable of satisfying this desire. But in wanting to be part of something "larger than themselves," what exactly is it that people want? Part of the answer is that they want to be participants in an agential enterprise that includes other people in addition to themselves and whose overall value exceeds, or differs in kind from, the value of any activities in which they might engage on their own. Although there are different ways in which an enterprise can be "larger" in the relevant respects, one important way is by being temporally ongoing. Ongoing group activities are larger than oneself not only in the sense that they include multiple agents, so that they transcend the limits of one's individual agential capacities, but also in the sense that they have a history and a future that are more extensive than one's own history and future, so that they transcend the temporal boundaries of one's personal existence. In consequence, the value of these ongoing group activities is not constrained, in the way the value of our purely individual activities is, either by the limitations of our individual talent or intelligence or will or by the temporal limits of our lifespans.

Many individual activities derive part of their value from the fact that, when one engages in the activity, one participates in a valuable ongoing enterprise of this kind. This does not mean that one's individual activity would have no value at all if it were a purely solitary endeavor and lacked a participatory character. It means only that, when it does have a participatory character, part of its value derives from that fact. The value of one's own individual activity is then intensified or augmented by its relation to the valuable, ongoing enterprise. Something like this is true, of course, with respect to the long-term, goal-oriented activities that I have already discussed, such as engaging in cancer research or political activism aimed at long-term reform. The individual cancer researcher's efforts are much more valuable because they are part of an ongoing collaborative research project than they would be if they were isolated undertakings. But much the same is true of many activities that lack this type of goal-oriented structure. And it is noteworthy that, in many of these cases, the participatory character of one's individual efforts does not depend on their having causal efficacy. One can participate in an ongoing enterprise, in the relevant sense, and one's activities can share in the value of that larger enterprise, even if one has no significant causal impact on the future of the enterprise.

Consider, to begin with an example close to home, the activity of producing works of philosophy. People who engage in this activity are participants in an ongoing collaborative process of inquiry. They are not solipsistic scribblers laboring at private diaries. They are captivated by questions that others have asked, formulating their thoughts in the light of what others have said, and expressing their ideas in anticipation of further inquiry to come. The value of what they do derives in part from its participatory character and from the value of the ongoing collaborative process in which it makes them participants. Similar things could be said, I believe, about many other valuable activities: from science to politics to literature to journalism to the exploration of the natural world to technological innovation to religious devotion to organized athletic competition. It may be difficult even to imagine some of these activities taking place as isolated, synchronic endeavors—as ephemeral, one-off manifestations of idiosyncratic purposiveness—but to the extent that we succeed in thinking of them that way they do not seem nearly as valuable. This is something that people implicitly recognize when they talk about being part of something larger than themselves. And it explains why one good-making feature of many individual activities is the specific feature of belonging to a valuable ongoing practice or process. This is a good-making feature because it confers on the individual activities in question a kind of value, or a degree of value, that they would not otherwise have. But that value would be compromised if the destruction of humanity were imminent, for then the valuable practices and processes would no longer be ongoing in the relevant sense.

The second additional good-making feature that many valuable activities have is the feature of helping to sustain a valuable heritage and so to preserve and enrich the cultural, practical, and intellectual resources available to our successors. What is relevant here is not the participatory character of these activities but rather the way they sustain and transmit valuable forms of human wisdom, practice, and achievement to new generations that might otherwise lose them. This is true, for example, of many educational, curatorial, and conservation-oriented activities. It is true of many activities undertaken with the explicit aim of preserving, sustaining, or enriching a cultural, intellectual, or religious tradition. And it is true of many activities involving the inculcation and transmission of valuable skills, crafts, and practical excellences. All these activities would be diminished in value by humanity's imminent extinction, for the impending catastrophe would eliminate the possibility of the kind of intergenerational transmission that makes them so valuable.

Finally, many activities have among their implicit good-making features the specific feature of helping us to make sense of our social world and its future possibilities. This is true, for example, of activities such as reading, studying, and teaching works of history, political theory, sociology, and anthropology. It is also true of many forms of engagement with the arts, whether as a producer or as a consumer. The point is not that the value of creating art, or of engaging with art that others have created, derives from the hope or expectation, even if well-founded, that the artworks themselves will survive long into the future, still less from the thought or fantasy that their extended longevity might somehow have the knock-on effect of extending one's own. The point is rather that part of the value that art has for us derives from the way it works to stimulate and to inform our imaginative reflections about the future: whether our own, society's, or humanity's. In this respect, there is a perhaps surprising overlap between the value of art and the value of learning about history, politics, social organization, and the practices of different cultures. All these activities are valuable in part because they can help us to think better—more creatively, more insightfully, more imaginatively—about human societies and the possibilities open to them. To truncate humanity's future is, therefore, to diminish the value of all of them.

I have treated these three good-making features as independent of one another, but of course they often go together. The artist

Vincent Desiderio, whose painting "Sleep" was the inspiration for a video by Kanye West, was quoted as saying, in response to the question of whether he had granted legal permission for West to refer to his painting: "As far as I'm concerned, it has nothing to do with copyright. A work of art goes out there, and there's a stream that activates and widens the communal imagination. It was an honor that I was being quoted. There was no money involved at all."[9] Desiderio's reply helps to illustrate, with respect to the activities associated with artistic creativity and engagement in particular, the way the three good-making features can go together. I have said that the arts inform our imaginative understanding of our social world and its possibilities, thus illustrating the third of the three features. But, as Desiderio's reply suggests, it is equally true that artistic activity derives part of its value from the way it sustains and enriches cultural traditions: traditions that are inherited, reproduced, challenged, reimagined, and modified by each generation, before being transmitted in more or less altered form to the next generation. This means that artistic activity has the second feature—the feature of sustaining and transmitting a valuable heritage—as well as the third. And, of course, Desiderio's comment makes clear that such activity also has the first feature. It derives part of its value from the fact that it belongs to an ongoing collaborative process: the ongoing collaborative work of the human imagination.

I have been arguing that the value of many of our activities depends, to a degree that we do not always recognize or acknowledge, on the survival of humanity long after we ourselves are gone. This reflects a more general fact about our values and concerns, which is that they have an important diachronic dimension. When

---

[9] Joe Coscarelli, "The Artist Providing the Canvas for Kanye West's 'Famous' Video," *The New York Times*, June 29, 2016, p. C3.

we engage in valuable activities, we follow in others' footsteps, fill their shoes, struggle with their legacies, learn from their mistakes, and stand on their shoulders to see further. We also break new ground, blaze new trails, make new mistakes, and create histories and legacies of our own. Eventually, we pass the torch, or the baton, to a new generation. Our concerns are pervasively diachronic, and one cannot fully appreciate the value of our activities without appreciating their diachronic dimension and the way it contributes to their value.[10]

But suppose I am right in arguing that the value of many of our activities depends on the survival of humanity after we ourselves are gone. What exactly does this show? The broad tendency of the argument, it may seem, is to suggest that we have self-interested reasons to ensure humanity's survival. We need future generations to survive in order that we ourselves can lead what I call "value-laden lives": lives structured by wholehearted engagement in valuable activities. If so, then it appears to follow that our reasons for trying to ensure the survival of future generations are purely self-interested reasons that derive ultimately from our concern for ourselves.

In *Death and the Afterlife*, unfortunately, I tacitly encouraged this interpretation even though I explicitly disavowed it. I tacitly encouraged it because I maintained that there is a specific sense in which the survival of humanity after our own deaths matters more to us than our personal survival. The point was that, however terrified we may be at the prospect of our own deaths, the prospect

---

[10] The diachronic character of our concerns is an important theme of Janna Thompson's thoughtful book *Intergenerational Justice* (New York: Routledge, 2009). She introduces the notion of a person's "lifetime-transcending interests," and makes use of that notion to develop a theory of justice between generations.

of humanity's imminent extinction would actually do more to undermine our capacity, here and now, to find value in our activities. This may naturally be taken to mean that the only reason we need humanity to survive is in order to fulfill our own interest in leading valuable lives. At the same time, I explicitly disavowed this interpretation. I claimed that the fact that the prospect of humanity's extinction would be so devastating for us reveals some *limits* to our egoism, because it reveals the extent to which we are dependent on the survival of others—indeed, on the coming into existence of as yet nonexistent strangers—in order to find value in our own lives. But without denying this point about our dependence on others, some readers have continued to feel that, insofar as this line of thought shows that we have reasons for seeking to ensure the survival of humanity, those reasons are nevertheless purely self-interested ones, because they have their source in our concern to lead valuable lives ourselves. Humanity's survival matters to us only because our confidence that it will survive is a precondition for our finding value in our own projects and goals.[11]

---

[11] See, for example, David Owens's review of *Death and the Afterlife* in *The Times Literary Supplement* of February 21, 2014, p. 21. Owens writes: "Scheffler has given the selfish person no reason to value the continuance of humanity for its own sake. The selfish person needs human beings to serve as partners in their projects and as an appreciative audience for their achievements. The future existence of other human beings is a means to such selfish ends. The survival of humanity need have no significance of its own, no worth which might be weighed in the balance against our personal interests. It is simply a precondition for anything to matter to us." Similarly, Amia Srinivasan, reviewing *Death and the Afterlife* in the *London Review of Books* of September 25, 2014 (pp. 13–14), takes the point of the argument to be "that there is a sense in which our own self-interest is better served by the preservation of the human species than by our personal survival or the survival of our loved ones."

Yet from the fact that our confidence in the value of our projects depends on our belief that humanity will survive after we are gone, it does not follow that humanity's survival matters to us only or primarily for that reason. It does not follow, nor do I believe it is true. If the human race were faced with imminent extinction through, for example, universal infertility, then, as I have said, many people would view this as a terrible catastrophe. They would find it emotionally devastating. The prospect of humanity's imminent disappearance would lead to widespread grief, gloom, and depression. The fact that people would react this way shows not that they think humanity's disappearance would be a setback to their interests but rather that the survival of humanity matters to them in its own right. Indeed, the very fact that humanity's survival matters to them in its own right is the most basic reason its disappearance would be a setback to their interests.

To be sure, I have also been arguing that many activities would become less valuable, and that others would lose their value altogether, if the disappearance of humanity were imminent. Some of the most obvious examples, as we have seen, are provided by long-term, goal-oriented projects with meliorative aims. The imminent extinction of humanity would make many of these activities pointless, and so it would be instrumentally irrational for people to continue to engage in them. Why bother trying to find a cure for cancer, or to enhance the seismic safety of bridges, or to improve the quality of early childhood education, if there will be nobody around to benefit from one's efforts? Since, under present conditions, the people engaged in these activities have an interest in continuing to engage in them, the disappearance of humanity would deliver an additional setback to these people's interests. The same is true of all the many people whose projects or activities, whether meliorative or not, would diminish in value if humanity were about to disappear. Yet this additional setback, important as it is, should not be confused with the more basic setback to people's interests resulting from the defeat of their prior and independent concern for humanity's survival.

In the case of the meliorative activities, there is a further point that deserves emphasis. The fact that many people think it antecedently worthwhile to engage in such activities, so that their interests eventually become bound up with the success of those activities, provides additional evidence that what happens to future generations matters to these people independently of their own interests. They believe it is worth devoting their lives to activities whose greatest benefits may not be realized until after they are gone. If they did not believe that, they would not choose to engage in such activities in the first place, and their interests would not come to be defined by them. In other words, the long-term meliorative activities take for granted the importance of what happens to future generations. Thus, with respect to people engaged in these activities in particular, we can say not only that it is because the survival of future generations matters to them in its own right that they would find the prospect of humanity's imminent extinction to be devastating, but also that the activities that help to define their interests make sense only on the assumption that the fate of future generations already matters to them.

Of course, many activities whose value would be compromised by the imminent extinction of humanity do not have a long-term, meliorative structure. Yet some of these activities also make sense only on the assumption that what happens to future generations matters to the participants. Consider, for example, activities aimed at ensuring the intergenerational transmission of valuable knowledge, traditions, or skills. If people who engage in these activities did not think it was important for future generations to have access to the relevant forms of knowledge and practice, they would not think it worth devoting their lives to trying to ensure such access. And although a parallel observation may not apply to all the activities whose value would be compromised by humanity's imminent extinction, the more general and fundamental point still holds: insofar as we would experience the imminent disappearance of humanity as devastating, the primary reason is not that it would be a setback to our interests but rather that the survival of humanity matters to us in its own right. If the survival of human beings did not already matter to us, we would not have as great an interest in trying to ensure it.[12] In short, we have an interest in their survival in part because they matter to us; they do not matter to us solely because we have an interest in their survival.[13]

Granted, this may not be true of everyone. Suppose that my only project in life is to build large monuments to myself so that future generations of human beings will know who I was and think about me from time to time. Then a belief that humanity will survive is necessary in order for me to find value in my project, and the imminent extinction of the human race would deprive the project of its point, but humanity's survival may not matter to me in any other way. It may matter to me only insofar as it is a precondition

---

[12] The argument here is in the spirit of Hume's discussion, in Appendix II of the *Enquiry Concerning the Principles of Morals*, of the need for motives "antecedent to self-love."

[13] On this structural point I am broadly in agreement with Wallace, "Value, Trauma, and the Future of Humanity," although his account of why exactly human survival matters to us omits the consideration I have been emphasizing, which is our direct concern for humanity itself. Wallace thinks that what we are directly concerned about, insofar as we are concerned with human survival, is the survival of our values. As I indicate in Chapter Three, I too think that is an important part of the story, but it is not the only part.

for finding value in my project. But this is an unusual case for several reasons. It is unusual, in part, because most people do not seriously hope or expect that they will be remembered by future generations at all. It is also unusual because, for most people who do wish to be remembered by future generations, the wish is not simply to be remembered, but to be remembered because one has done something worthy of recognition and admiration. With respect to these people, then, we need to ask what activities or accomplishments they regard as worthy of admiration and how the value of those activities and accomplishments would be affected by the imminent extinction of humanity. Finally, the case I have described is unusual because most people who wish to be remembered by future generations have many other aims and motives as well, and they are no less likely than anyone else to have a direct concern for the survival of humanity. Once these considerations are taken into account, the wider implications of the case are bound to seem quite limited.

It may appear that my argument has an elitist character, because only those who are relatively affluent and well-educated can devote themselves to activities whose value depends on the assumption that humanity will survive. Most people don't have the luxury of devoting themselves to such activities; they must work at unrewarding jobs, if they can find them, simply so that they themselves can survive. The value of these unrewarding activities would not be undermined by the prospect of humanity's imminent disappearance. But rather than refuting my argument, this consideration reinforces it. It is true that relatively few people have the luxury of earning their living by engaging in activities they find independently rewarding. It is a privilege to be able to support oneself as a scientist or an artist or an athlete or an intellectual, or by performing any other type of labor that is intrinsically rewarding. But the fact that many people must work at unrewarding activities in order to survive—activities they do not independently value—tells us nothing about the character of the activities people do value or find rewarding. In particular, it does not show that the survival of future generations matters only to the rich or the privileged; it shows only that the rich and the privileged are more likely to be able to devote their lives to independently valuable activities. And it is only when our activities reflect our values that they are good indicators of what matters to us. We should find it striking that the more people have the resources that make it possible for them to choose rewarding activities to which to devote themselves, the more they gravitate toward endeavors that depend for their point on the assumption that humanity will persist.

The upshot is that, in addition to any reasons of beneficence we may have, we also have reasons of two further kinds to attach significance to the fate of future generations. The first, which we may call reasons of concern, rest on the fact that their fate matters to us in its own right, while the second, which we may call reasons of interest, appeal to our own interest in leading lives engaged in worthwhile activities. These two categories of reason are conceptually independent, but it is partly because the fate of future generations matters to us in its own right that their survival is in our interest.

These conclusions, it should be emphasized, do not depend on the truth of my claim that many of our activities would diminish in value if the extinction of humanity were imminent. Suppose that, contrary to what I have argued, the fact that our activities would seem to us less valuable in those circumstances is best interpreted as an evaluative mistake produced by intense grief and depression. Nevertheless, the very fact that we would react to the prospect of human extinction with intense grief and depression testifies to our direct concern for humanity's survival. And the fact that we have such a concern, and that its frustration would produce disabling grief and depression, means that we also have an interest in human survival. So even if our reaction to the prospect of humanity's disappearance did involve an evaluative mistake, we would still have reasons of both types to care about the fate of future generations.

There is a lot packed into the thought that the survival of humanity or of future generations matters to us in its own right. As I said in Chapter One, the idea of future generations is the idea of a succession of cohorts, each related to its predecessors and successors both temporally and causally, extending from now into the future. Similarly, the idea of humanity's survival is not just the idea of human beings existing sometime in the future. It is the idea that, for a good long time at least, there will continue to be human beings who are causally related in familiar ways both to those who came before them and to those who will come after them. Insofar as the fate of future generations matters to us, and insofar as we care about the survival of humanity, what matters to us is that the causal and temporal chain of generations should continue. Nor are we concerned solely with humanity's bare survival. Rather, we want future generations to survive under conditions conducive to their flourishing. This is not a concern about the "welfare" of future people considered as an unstructured group. What we are concerned about is the extension of the chain of human generations through time.

Since the chain of generations is constituted ultimately by chains of individual descent, you might think that any concern we have for the former must reduce to a concern for some instances of the latter. You might think, for example, that our concern for future generations consists in a concern that we ourselves should have children, who in turn have children, and so on into the indefinite future. But this is a mistake. Many people do, of course, have an intense desire to have children, and many have a very strong desire to have grandchildren. Some people, though fewer, have a strong desire that their own line of descent should continue indefinitely into the future. But the concern that the chain of human generations should extend into the future is not a concern that some particular line of individual descent should persist. The two desires are not mutually exclusive, of course, but the one does not reduce to the other. Dismay at the prospect of humanity's imminent extinction would not be limited to those who have or expect to have children, so it is not only those who have or expect to have children to whom the fate of future generations matters.

Similarly, our concern for future generations is not a concern that we as individuals should be remembered after we die. That too is a desire that many people have, although in most cases it is primarily a desire to be remembered by some of the people one knew personally, and since those people will themselves exist only for a limited time, the temporal scope of the desire is relatively modest. There are, as we have seen, some people who hope to be remembered into the further future for their achievements, but they are many fewer in number, and in even fewer cases is the hope at all realistic. But these hopes and desires, whether more or less modest, are independent of the concern I am describing, which is a concern that humanity should survive and should flourish, and not a concern that one should oneself be remembered.

Finally, the concern for future generations does not consist in or reduce to a desire to have some impact on the lives of one's successors. Again, many people do hope to do something during their lifetimes that will have some positive effect on those who come after them. That much is clear from the prevalence of the meliorative research projects and the forms of social and political activism that I discussed earlier. But the concern for future generations is presupposed by, and does not reduce to, a hope or wish of this kind, still less to a hope or wish that future generations should survive *in order that* one may have a positive impact on their lives.

Our concern for future generations is at once more straightforward and apparently more mysterious. It is straightforward because it is simply a concern that the chain of human generations should be extended into the indefinite future under conditions conducive to human flourishing. What makes this concern seem mysterious is what I have called our temporal parochialism. Most of us lack any clear or well-developed conception of the value of human continuity or of the values that we hope will be realized in the future. Nor do we exhibit any normatively articulate understanding of the importance to us of future generations or of our own relations to them. If I am right, though, our concern for future generations gives the lie to, or at any rate shows the limits of, our temporal parochialism. When, in imagination, we contemplate the imminent disappearance of the human race, and when we react to that prospect with feelings of loss and sadness and even despair, we make it clear that, despite our tendency to overlook the fact, the survival of human beings matters deeply to us. The point can be put more strongly. Suppose we agree that love is an evaluative attitude that represents its objects in a favorable light and includes a strong concern for their flourishing. And suppose we agree that to love a person is, among other things, to be vulnerable to a wide range of context-dependent emotions, including, most notably, distress if the person is harmed or damaged or destroyed. So too, *mutatis mutandis*, when what we love is not a person but something else. Then we may add that, in reacting as we do to the prospect of humanity's imminent disappearance, what we reveal is our love of humanity.[14]

---

[14] On the relations among love, evaluation, and emotional vulnerability, see Niko Kolodny, "Love as Valuing a Relationship," *Philosophical Review*

This may seem preposterous. How can we be said to love people whose identities are unknown, who don't yet exist, who may never in fact exist, and who, if they do exist, won't do so until after we are dead? How can it even be said that we are concerned about these nonexistent people or that they matter to us? Surely the indeterminacy of their identities and our uncertainty about whether they will ever exist are incompatible with attitudes like love and concern. But this is a mistake. To be sure, the love of humanity differs from the love of particular people we know, just as a love of literature differs from the love of one's dog. In general, love varies as its objects vary. The love of humanity does not consist in a love of future individuals as individuals. Instead, it comprehends a range of attitudes and dispositions. These include a deep desire that the chain of human generations should extend into the indefinite future under conditions conducive to human flourishing, and a disposition to emotions like profound sadness at the prospect of humanity's imminent disappearance. None of these desires or dispositions is rendered irrational or inappropriate by our lack of knowledge of the identities of the particular people who will live in the future or even by uncertainty about whether they will exist at all.

The suggestion that we exhibit a love of humanity may strike some people as preposterous for a different reason. Even though I have not suggested that this form of love is universal, but only

---

112(2003): 135–89. I have discussed the relation between valuing and vulnerability in "Valuing" (included in my *Equality and Tradition* [New York: Oxford University Press, 2010], pp. 15–40) and in "Projects, Relationships, and Reasons" (in R. Jay Wallace, Philip Pettit, Samuel Scheffler, and Michael Smith, eds., *Reason and Value: Themes from the Moral Philosophy of Joseph Raz* [Oxford: Clarendon Press, 2004], pp. 247–69). On the same point, see also Elizabeth Anderson, *Value in Ethics and Economics* (Cambridge, MA: Harvard University Press, 1993), chapter 1.

that it is very widespread, it may seem that in order to refute the suggestion one has only to read the newspaper: any newspaper, anywhere in the world, on any given day. The ongoing record of human savagery, brutality, and violence is so overwhelming, and these tendencies of human behavior manifest themselves with such depressing frequency and on such a staggering scale, that one would have to be mad to propose that a love of humanity is a significant feature of human psychology. Yet the prevalence of human savagery does not undermine the reality of human love, any more than the prevalence of cruelty undermines the reality of kindness or the prevalence of greed undermines the reality of generosity. In suggesting that many people would react to the prospect of imminent human extinction with sadness and even despair, and that these attitudes reveal a form of concern that might best be described as a love of humanity, I am not suggesting that this concern is our only concern or our strongest concern or a concern that coheres smoothly with every other aspect of our psychologies. The complexity of human attitudes and motivations is their most striking feature, which is why every simplifying and reductive theory of human psychology inevitably ends in failure. We human beings are a strange and wondrous and terrible species. Our motives are nothing if not mixed. What I have called the love of humanity is simply part of the mix.

The love of humanity should not be confused with the motive of sympathy, which plays such a central role in utilitarian moral psychology. Sympathy, as utilitarians understand it, is a disposition to identify with the pleasures and pains of others, and an ideally sympathetic spectator, as conceptualized by utilitarian theorists, would identify equally with all of the individuals affected by a given act or institution. By contrast, the love of humanity, as I have defined it, includes a desire that the chain of human generations should extend into the indefinite future under conditions that are conducive to human flourishing. This desire is not equivalent to a form of idealized sympathy, and although the practical implications of the two motives may sometimes coincide, this need not always be the case.

Some people may think that the love of humanity is reducible not to sympathy but rather to self-interest. They may say that what I have called reasons of concern, or what we might instead call reasons of love, are themselves self-interested reasons.[15] They are reasons to care about future generations only because future generations matter *to us*. But this is specious. One might just as well say that our reasons for acting in behalf of the particular people we love, or for concerning ourselves with their well-being, are self-interested, since we have such reasons only because these people matter to us. This is a mistake, albeit a common one, for it neglects the distinction between the interests of a self and an interest in oneself.[16] When we are distressed because someone we love has been harmed, or because something we value greatly has been damaged or destroyed, the fact that it is we who care about the person or value the thing does not make our distress self-interested. To say that we are self-interested is to say something about what we take

---

[15] In *The Reasons of Love* (Princeton, NJ: Princeton University Press, 2004), Harry Frankfurt uses the phrase "reasons of love" in roughly the same sense that I am using it here, although I am applying it specifically to our love of humanity and I am not relying on Frankfurt's volitional interpretation of love. Susan Wolf also employs Frankfurt's phrase in her *Meaning in Life and Why It Matters* (Princeton, NJ: Princeton University Press, 2010).

[16] See John Rawls, *A Theory of Justice* (Cambridge, MA: Harvard University Press, 1971), section 22.

an interest in, namely, ourselves. It is not to say that it is we who take an interest.

There is another suggestion about the relation between reasons of love and self-interested reasons that is more plausible. The real significance of our reaction to the prospect of humanity's imminent extinction, it may be said, is that it reveals the superficiality of the distinction between these two types of reason. When we reflect carefully about our reaction to the prospect of humanity's destruction, we come to realize two complementary things. The first is that, because we implicitly understand our own lives as situated at a particular location within a temporally ordered succession of human lives, a threat to the survival of that order is also a threat to us and to the significance of our lives. So insofar as we take a genuine interest in the quality and significance of our lives, that interest must itself encompass a concern for the lives of our successors. The second is that our profound sadness and sense of loss in the face of humanity's imminent destruction registers in part as a shock to ourselves, as an assault on our understanding of our own place in the world. So insofar as we are genuinely concerned with the fate of future generations—insofar as we exhibit a real love of humanity—our love and concern must themselves encompass a recognition of the damage that is done to us when humanity is destroyed. If these observations are correct, then it is a mistake to treat reasons of interest and reasons of love as two separate categories. The real force of the considerations we have been discussing is to show how artificial that distinction is. Properly understood, our interest in ourselves and our concern for what happens to our successors are inseparable. Self-interest and the love of humanity cannot be so neatly pried apart.

There is much truth in this line of thought, but it doesn't deprive the distinction between reasons of interest and reasons of love of all its value. Notwithstanding the deep interconnections between our interest in ourselves, as we may come to understand it upon reflection, and our concern for what happens to our successors, we can still distinguish between the fact that the imminent extinction of humanity would produce in us a direct and immediate sense of loss and the fact that it would defeat many of our own interests. And it is important to see that the first fact is not explained by but rather helps to explain the second. Since the distinction between reasons of love and reasons of interest provides an effective way of making this point, I will continue to employ that distinction.

CHAPTER THREE

Reasons to Worry: Valuation and Reciprocity

I argued in Chapter Two that we have reasons of at least two different kinds, apart from reasons of beneficence, for concerning ourselves with the fate of future generations: reasons of love and reasons of interest. Reasons of love are rooted in our direct concern for the survival of humanity. Reasons of interest derive from our fundamental interest in leading lives of value here and now, an interest that would be compromised, in more than one way, by the prospect of humanity's imminent disappearance. But our reactions to that prospect reveal reasons of another kind as well, for part of the dismay we feel in contemplating the human race's imminent extinction is a response neither to the defeat of our own interests nor to the fate of the humanity we love, but rather to the destruction of many of the other things that we value.

As I emphasized in *Death and the Afterlife*, there is a conservative dimension to valuing, something approaching a conceptual connection between valuing something and wanting it to be sustained and to persist over time.[1] In general, we are not indifferent to the destruction of the things that we value; we are not indifferent as

---

[1] I had previously discussed this connection in "Immigration and the Significance of Culture," *Philosophy & Public Affairs* 35(2007): 93–125,

between their survival and their disappearance. Admittedly, our conservatism is, as Seana Shiffrin has pointed out, a complex phenomenon.[2] In some cases, what we want to survive are particular token items that we value: works of art, beautiful buildings, personal relationships. In other cases, what we want to survive are types rather than tokens: wonderful meals, beautiful concerts, thrilling conversations. We don't want individual instances of these types to last forever, but we do want the types to continue to be instantiated. It is also true that we value some things that are essentially ephemeral: bonfires, sandcastles, shooting stars. And our conservatism is in some tension with other attitudes that we hold. In addition to wanting to sustain the things we already value, for example, we also want to create new forms of value and new items of value. We are not only conservative but also creative creatures, and sometimes our conservative impulses clash with our creative ones.[3] Yet all this is by way of qualification rather than refutation. In general, there is a strong connection between valuing something and wanting it to be sustained and preserved over time.

This connection helps to explain part of our reaction to the prospect of humanity's imminent disappearance, for part of what is shocking about that prospect is the recognition of how much of what we value will disappear along with the human race. All of the many things we value that consist in or depend on forms of human

reprinted in *Equality and Tradition*, pp. 256–86, and in "The Normativity of Tradition," *Equality and Tradition*, pp. 287–311.

[2] See Seana Shiffrin, "Preserving the Valued or Preserving Valuing?," in Scheffler, *Death and the Afterlife* (New York: Oxford University Press, 2013), pp. 143–58. My discussion in this paragraph and the one that follows is deeply indebted to Shiffrin's essay.

[3] Although, as I will argue in Chapter Five, it is an important fact that the two impulses do not always conflict.

activity will be lost when human beings become extinct. No more beautiful singing or graceful dancing or intimate friendship or warm family celebrations or hilarious jokes or gestures of kindness or displays of solidarity. Other things that we value—physical artifacts, for example—may survive for a while, but with no one to appreciate their value, for in addition to the disappearance of *valuable things*, the extinction of the human race will mean the disappearance of *valuing* from the Earth. Whether value can survive without valuing—whether it makes sense to speak of the existence of value in a world where there is nobody left to value anything—is a nice question for philosophers, but for the purpose of understanding our reactions to the prospect of humanity's imminent extinction the answer doesn't matter very much. When we contemplate that prospect with horror or dismay, part of what we are registering is the disappearance of vast numbers of things that we value along with the entire known realm of beings with the capacity to appreciate value. And our horror at this prospect points to another reason why the fate of future generations matters to us: it matters to us because, in the respects just mentioned, the future of humanity is the future of value. This means that, in addition to reasons of love and reasons of interest, we have reasons of a third kind, which I will call *reasons of valuation*, to concern ourselves with the fate of future generations. What is at issue here is neither our direct concern for humanity nor our interest in being able to engage in valued activities during our lifetimes. What is at issue is our desire that the things that we value—and the very phenomenon of valuing things—should survive into the future.[4]

---

[4] The role of this desire in explaining our reaction to the prospect of humanity's imminent extinction is emphasized by Wallace, "Value, Trauma, and the Future of Humanity," as well as by Shiffrin.

I want now to suggest, finally, that we also have reasons of still another kind for taking the interests of future generations seriously, namely, *reasons of reciprocity*. Let me clarify what I mean by this. When people speak of reciprocity in the intergenerational context, often what they mean is that we have reasons to "pay it forward," or to benefit the next generation in the ways that we ourselves were benefited (or should have been benefited) by the previous generation. This is sometimes described as a principle of reciprocity in an extended sense, or as a principle of indirect reciprocity, or as something that resembles a principle of reciprocity. Consider, for example, Samuel Freeman's remarks, when discussing a version of the principle that we should benefit our successors in the same ways that we would have wanted our predecessors to benefit us. Freeman writes: "While this is not a principle of reciprocity—after all, future generations are not able to reciprocate the benefits we bestow on them by bestowing benefits on us—it resembles a principle of reciprocity in that it says in effect: 'Do unto future generations as you would have previous generations do unto you.'"[5,6] However plausible this principle may be, it is not what I have in mind when I talk about reasons of reciprocity. I mean instead to be suggesting something that may initially sound much less plausible, namely, that we stand in relations of genuine mutual dependence with future

---

[5] Samuel Freeman, *Rawls* (Abingdon: Routledge, 2007), p. 139.

[6] On the important idea of "indirect reciprocity," see Axel Gosseries, "Three Models of Intergenerational Reciprocity," in A. Gosseries and L. Meyer, eds., *Intergenerational Justice* (Oxford: Oxford University Press, 2009), pp. 119–46. For a cogent defense of the idea that systems of indirect reciprocity can and do exist intergenerationally, see Joseph Heath, "The Structure of Intergenerational Cooperation," *Philosophy & Public Affairs* 41(2013): 31–66.

generations and that it is in virtue of those relations that we have reasons of reciprocity for taking their interests seriously.

How can this possibly be? Our relations to future generations seem far too asymmetrical to count as relations of reciprocity.[7] After all, our successors are causally dependent on us. We have the power to affect what happens to them during their lifetimes in profound ways. Indeed, we have the power to determine whether they will live at all. It's not just that we have the power to affect how many of them will live and what quality of life those who live will enjoy. More radically, we have the power to determine whether human life itself will continue. By contrast, we are not causally dependent on our successors in these same ways. If and when they come into existence, they will not be able retroactively to determine whether we have lived or to exert a causal influence on what happened to us during our lifetimes.

Of course, this does not mean that what they end up doing should strike us prospectively as a matter of indifference. After all, they may bring about or frustrate the posthumous fulfillment of our desires. They may determine whether we are remembered or forgotten, praised or blamed, honored or despised. They may describe our activities fairly, unfairly, or not at all. They may build on our achievements or they may destroy them. They may even make true certain descriptions of what happened to us during our lifetimes. For example, people born after your death may make it true that, during your lifetime, you were befriended by the great-great-grandmother of a mass murderer or a Nobel-Prize winning physicist. These observations may be taken to show that, even though future generations

---

[7] This point is forcefully argued by Brian Barry in "Justice Between Generations," in Hacker and Raz, eds., *Law, Morality and Society: Essays in Honour of H.L.A. Hart* (Oxford: Clarendon Press, 1977).

cannot have a causal impact on what happens to us during our lifetimes, there are nevertheless respects in which we are dependent on them. But in saying that we have reasons of reciprocity for taking their fate seriously, I mean to be pointing to a more fundamental kind of dependence. If what I said earlier is correct, we are dependent on future generations not merely for the reasons just given but also because our confidence in the value of our current activities implicitly depends on our confidence in their survival, and the actual value of many of our activities does in fact depend on their survival. We are, in this sense, evaluatively dependent on them. And we are emotionally dependent on them as well, inasmuch as the prospect of humanity's imminent disappearance would be profoundly distressing to us. This means that there is a distinctive kind of mutual dependence that characterizes our relations with future generations. On the one hand, the quality of their lives and their very existence are causally dependent on what we do. On the other hand, we are evaluatively and emotionally dependent on them and their survival.

In view of this mutual dependence, there is room for a certain idea of reciprocity, which I will call *evaluative reciprocity*, to govern our relations to future generations. The prospect of their survival is a precondition for, and so contributes to, our being able to lead value-laden lives. At the same time, there are many different ways in which we can enhance their ability to lead good lives in the future. Because of these reciprocal relations, we have reasons of reciprocity, which go beyond the reasons of love, interest, and valuation already discussed, to concern ourselves with their fate.

But what exactly is meant by saying that the prospect of their survival is a precondition for our being able to lead value-laden lives? There are two sides to this idea. First, it means that our *belief* in their survival is a causal precondition both of our emotional equanimity and of our confidence in the value of our activities. But second, it means that their survival *itself* underwrites the actual value of many of our activities and, in so doing, provides us with *reasons* for confidence in the value of those activities. It is the fact of their survival that is reason-giving, not our belief in that fact. This is something that we ourselves implicitly recognize, for if we knew that they would not survive, then the prospect of taking a drug that would induce in us a false belief in their survival would be small consolation. We would not suppose that the actual value of our activities was about to be restored.

This characterization of the way in which future generations contribute to our ability to lead value-laden lives is important. The suggestion that an idea of reciprocity applies to our relations to future generations may seem like a non-starter if we assume, as Samuel Freeman implicitly does in the passage I quoted, that in a relationship of reciprocity, the reciprocal contribution of each party to the other must be understood in terms of the causal effects that each has on the life of the other. Clearly, generations who exist at some future time cannot make causal contributions to our well-being now. At most it is the prospect of their existence, which is to say our belief that they will exist, that can make such contributions. However, the idea of evaluative reciprocity, as applied to the case of future generations, asserts something different. It asserts that, on the one hand, we can causally enhance the ability of future generations to lead good and worthwhile lives. But, on the other hand, their survival enhances in a different way our ability to lead lives of purpose and value. Their most important contribution to us is not causal but rational, because their survival provides us with reasons for confidence in the value of many of our activities. As I have argued, this is what we ourselves believe, since if we thought they would not survive, we would see less reason to engage in many of the activities that we now value deeply.

Nevertheless, in view of the asymmetrical causal relations between us and future generations, some will continue to doubt whether what I have described is really a form of reciprocity. They will want to assert just what I am denying, namely, that in order for talk of reciprocity to be appropriate in this context, future generations would have to make some causal contribution to the quality of our lives. At first glance, this may seem like a mere terminological disagreement: a dispute about how the word "reciprocity" is to be used. As such, it may appear to be of little interest. However, there is more at stake here than a clash of terminological stipulations. The term "reciprocity" is appropriate in this context because our relation to future generations is one of genuine mutual dependence, even if the form taken by our dependence on them is different from the form taken by their dependence on us. Each side is dependent on, and so is vulnerable to, what the other does or what happens to the other. This makes it appropriate to speak of a relationship of reciprocity between them.[8]

---

[8] The asymmetrical character of this form of reciprocity has one striking consequence. If we ask what reasons of evaluative reciprocity tell us to do, then a very general answer is that they tell us to act in such a way as to enhance the likelihood that future generations will survive and flourish. But if we do that, then we will *eo ipso* be providing reasons for confidence that future generations will in fact survive and flourish, which is the condition that they must meet if our activities are to retain their value. This means that the very same conduct that constitutes our contribution to future generations also helps to secure their contribution to us. This is a consequence of the asymmetry between their causal dependence on us and our rational dependence on them. Some may see this as further evidence that the term *reciprocity* is inappropriate in this case. I take it instead as a welcome feature of this form of reciprocity.

This terminology is appropriate for another reason as well. My primary aim in this book is to consider what reasons we have for concerning ourselves with the fate of future generations, but much of the interest of that theoretical question derives from its connection to the practical question of what might actually motivate us to address the serious threats now facing our descendants. As a general matter, reasons of reciprocity are often seen as a particularly powerful source of motivation. In *A Theory of Justice*, for example, John Rawls argues that there is a deep human tendency to reciprocate the love of others and the concern they display for one's well-being, and that this tendency plays a crucial developmental role in the long process that leads, under favorable conditions, to the eventual emergence in adult human beings of mature moral motivation. His arguments against utilitarianism importantly depend on the idea that his principles of justice are themselves reciprocity principles, which is to say that they embody an idea of reciprocity in their content. As such, they can draw on sources of motivation that are especially powerful and robust, in part because they are psychologically continuous with the developmentally most primitive forms of moral motivation. By contrast to the utilitarian reliance on sympathy as the primary basis for compliance, he maintains, his principles can appeal to the more stable and secure motive of reciprocity.[9]

In using the phrase "evaluative reciprocity" to characterize our relations with future generations, I mean to be suggesting that people who were sensitive to reasons of reciprocity of the usual kind would see reasons of a recognizably similar kind as applying to our relations with future generations, provided they understood

[9] Rawls, *A Theory of Justice* (Cambridge, MA: Harvard University Press, 1971; revised edition, 1999), sections 70–2, 75–6.

the kind of mutual dependence that characterizes those relations. The fact that people do not already acknowledge such reasons is not decisive evidence against this suggestion. It may show nothing more than that we have not yet been faced with the prospect of humanity's imminent extinction. Even people who, in their more reflective moments, harbor serious doubts about the future of humanity, nevertheless tend to assume, in the way they actually conduct their lives, that human beings will continue to inhabit the Earth for an indefinite period of time. Having taken the survival of humanity for granted, on a visceral if not on an intellectual level, we may never have had occasion to recognize how much it matters to us or how much we depend on it to support our confidence in the value of our own activities.

So my use of the term "evaluative reciprocity" rests on a conjecture that is at once psychological and conceptual. It rests on the conjecture that if people who were generally susceptible to considerations of reciprocity were to recognize the kind of mutual dependence that characterizes our relations to future generations, they would see those relations as giving rise to reasons for action in virtue of that mutual dependence. In other words, evaluative reciprocity would strike them as a kind of reciprocity. This is not a linguistic point. It does not mean that they would use the term "reciprocity" to characterize these perceived reasons for action—they might or might not. It means instead that considerations of evaluative reciprocity would engage the same motivational tendencies in them as considerations of ordinary causal reciprocity. It is this psychological and conceptual conjecture that underlies my use of the term "evaluative reciprocity" and renders it more than a metaphor or a mere terminological stipulation. And what is important, in the end, is the conjecture and not the terminology. If someone accepts the conjecture but insists on using a term other than "evaluative reciprocity" to refer to the phenomenon I am describing, then nothing of substance turns on this disagreement.

My suggestion, then, is that an idea of evaluative reciprocity governs our relations to future generations and that, in consequence, we have reasons of reciprocity to try to secure their survival and flourishing. It may seem that this suggestion gives rise to a version of Derek Parfit's "Non-Identity Problem."[10] In general, the non-identity problem arises when some action of ours seems wrong because of its effects on the lives of people in the future, and yet the particular people who are affected by that action would not even have existed if we had acted otherwise. Since their lives would not have gone better if we had refrained from the putatively objectionable action, how can that action be said to have wronged them? And if it did not wrong them, then why was it morally objectionable?

A version of this problem may seem to apply to reasons of reciprocity as I have described them. For suppose that we decide to ignore those purported reasons and that, in consequence, the quality of our successors' lives is much lower than the quality of our successors' lives would have been if we had not ignored those reasons and had acted otherwise. Yet if we had acted otherwise, our successors would have been different people (or so we may suppose). The particular people who in fact succeed us would not even have existed if we had not ignored our reasons of reciprocity. Since their lives would not have gone better if we had acted differently, how can what we have done be morally wrong?

---

[10] See Parfit, *Reasons and Persons* (Oxford: Clarendon Press, 1984), chapter 16. There is by now an enormous literature on this problem. Much of the literature to date is reviewed in David Boonin's painstaking book-length study, *The Non-Identity Problem and the Ethics of Future People* (Oxford: Oxford University Press, 2014).

However, I have not said that what we do if we disregard our reasons of reciprocity is morally wrong. Although, as I noted in my comments about Rawls, reciprocity is often seen as having an important role to play in moral motivation, I have not characterized the reasons of reciprocity I have been discussing as moral reasons, nor have I made any claim about the moral wrongness of disregarding those reasons. What I have characterized as reasons of reciprocity are reasons to try to secure the survival and flourishing of future generations. We have these reasons in virtue of the fact that their survival and flourishing give us reasons for confidence in the value of many of our activities. As I have already indicated, and as I will explain in greater detail in just a moment, it makes no difference to my argument whether we classify these reasons, or any of the other reasons I have been discussing, as moral reasons or not. What is important is simply that they are reasons with genuine normative force. And as far as the non-identity problem is concerned, the pertinent point is that neither the reasons for confidence that future generations give us nor our reciprocal reasons to try to ensure their survival and flourishing are dependent on the identities of the specific individuals who constitute those generations. So the fact that our failure to act on our reasons of reciprocity will result in different people being born is irrelevant. If we fail to act on those reasons, then we will not have tried to secure the survival and flourishing of future generations. We will not, in other words, have taken steps to ensure that each generation of human beings is succeeded by another generation whose circumstances are conducive to human flourishing. And that is what we have reason to do.

If I am right, then we have, apart from reasons of beneficence, reasons of at least four additional kinds to concern ourselves with the fate of future generations: reasons of love, reasons of interest, reasons of valuation, and reasons of reciprocity. As I said at the beginning of Chapter Two, I don't suppose that absolutely everyone has these reasons, only that many people do. Nor do I claim that these reasons are exhaustive of our non-beneficence-based reasons. Perhaps, for example, we also have reasons of "indirect reciprocity" of the kind that some writers have suggested.[11] And perhaps we have reasons of other kinds as well.[12] But reasons of the four kinds I have so far discussed belong to our collective repertoire of reasons. They are among the reasons that we the living have for seeking to secure the survival and flourishing of our descendants.

In Chapter One, I called attention to three limitations of the beneficence-based literature on problems of future generations. First, it encourages an overly moralized way of thinking about our relations to our successors, and makes it easier to neglect the broader evaluative significance that we attach to human survival and continuity. Second, even within the territory of morality, its preoccupation with duties of beneficence is unduly limiting and leads to a disproportionate emphasis on the puzzles of "population ethics." This narrows the focus of moral reflection and makes it easier to avoid asking whether there are other moral values and principles that have a bearing on our relations to our descendants. Indeed, in a puzzle-loving discipline like philosophy, the very difficulty of solving the puzzles of population ethics has only attracted more attention to the quest for solutions and so has further

[11] See the references cited in footnote 6 above.

[12] In his refreshingly heterodox though intermittently exasperating *How to Think Seriously about the Planet: The Case for an Environmental Conservatism* (New York: Oxford University Press, 2012), Roger Scruton argues forcefully for the importance of a motive he calls "oikophilia," by which he means a love of home. Scruton sees this motive as providing an insufficiently appreciated basis for concern both about the environment and about future generations.

discouraged people from considering a wider set of questions about the importance to us of the human future. Third, because of the extent to which beneficence-based duties as understood by those in the utilitarian tradition must rely on sympathy to motivate compliance, the beneficence-based literature provides little reason for optimism about the practical and especially the political prospects of effective action aimed at securing the survival of future generations.

Although I have expressed reservations about the role that a broadly utilitarian "principle of beneficence" should be expected to play in thinking about our responsibilities toward future generations, I don't mean to insist that reasons of beneficence have no role at all.[13] The four additional types of reason I have cited complement rather than exclude whatever reasons of beneficence there may be, and reflection on those additional reasons may help to overcome the three limitations of an exclusively beneficence-based approach.[14] Let me explain how.

First, as I have emphasized, I have not made any attempt to classify the reasons I have identified either as moral or as non-moral, nor have I drawn any conclusions couched in the language of moral duty. This may seem at first like a peculiarity of my discussion.

---

[13] In Chapter Four, I will suggest such a role.

[14] When I say that these four additional types of reason complement rather than exclude any reasons of beneficence there may be, I mean that one need not deny the existence of any one of these types of reason in order to affirm the others, and that people may in principle have reasons of all five kinds. I also assume that, as they apply to cases involving future generations, the different types of reason will in many cases support the same actions. But this is not to say that they can never give conflicting prescriptions for action. Perhaps, for example, there are cases in which reasons of beneficence, properly understood, will conflict with reasons of interest or reasons of valuation.

Surely, it may seem, we have moral obligations to our descendants, and that is the most obvious reason for concerning ourselves with their fates. But I have avoided couching my discussion in moral terms for two complementary reasons. On the one hand, the nature and extent of our moral obligations to our descendants is far from clear. Utilitarian accounts of those obligations are implausible and non-utilitarian accounts are underdeveloped. On the other hand, if we focus too single-mindedly on questions of obligation, we may fail to notice the remarkable diversity of reasons we have for caring about what happens to our descendants. We may create the impression, or reinforce it where it already exists, that the only reason we have for taking an interest in their fate is so that we can discharge our moral responsibilities. My aim in Chapters Two and Three has been to undercut this impression and to demonstrate that we have a whole set of reasons to care about future generations. For the purposes of this discussion, what matters is not whether these reasons are moral or non-moral but whether they are humanly recognizable and whether their normative force is clear. The pertinent point—the point I find illuminating and compelling—is that once we realize how much the future of humanity already matters to us, we can see that we possess reasons of a variety of kinds to help ensure the survival and flourishing of those who come after us. Perhaps some of these reasons should themselves be classified as moral reasons or perhaps we have moral reasons in addition to those I have canvassed. Given the aims of this discussion, it is not necessary to arrive at a settled assessment of these possibilities and so I will instead simply set them aside.

Second, since the reasons I have described are all independent of reasons of beneficence, they have no tendency to narrow the focus of investigation in the way that the beneficence-based literature does. Rather than directing our attention to the puzzles of population ethics in particular, they invite us to reflect in a more open-ended way about how the diverse considerations they exemplify might best be expressed in our actions and in the ways we choose to live.

Finally, there remains the question of how practical, political solutions might be found to the problems that threaten future generations. The four reasons I have described do not, of course, answer that question. They do not demonstrate what shape a politics of the future might take. But they do demonstrate that such a politics need not be left wholly at the mercy of the uncertain motivational power of sympathy. The reasons I have described—reasons of love, reasons of interest, reasons of valuation, and reasons of reciprocity—all have the potential to motivate action aimed at securing the survival and flourishing of future generations. What are needed are effective programs and strategies to achieve those aims. Of course, the task of creating such programs and strategies is bound to be challenging.[15] But the task is made needlessly difficult if we assume that utilitarian sympathy is the only motive that might be available to sustain any practical initiatives we undertake. Once we free ourselves from that assumption, we can see that, although the task of constructing an effective politics of the future represents a formidable challenge, there is no shortage of reasons or motives available to support such a politics. Insofar as there is a deficit that must be overcome if we

---

[15] For one interesting policy suggestion, see Thomas Wells, "Votes for the Future," *Aeon*, May 8, 2014. See also Dennis Thompson, "Representing Future Generations: Political Presentism and Democratic Trusteeship," *Critical Review of International Social and Political Philosophy* 13(2010): 17–37. For an encouraging empirical study of the potential for institutional solutions to problems of future generations, see Oliver P. Hauser, David G. Rand, Alexander Peysakhovich, and Martin A. Nowak, "Cooperating with the Future," *Nature* 511(July 10, 2014): 220–3.

are seriously to address the threats facing future generations, the deficit is as much political as it is motivational.

Still, the conclusions for which I have argued may seem disappointing when viewed through the lens of the beneficence-based literature on future generations. Rather than offering an alternative principle or set of principles that might play a role comparable to that of a principle of beneficence, all I have done is to identify reasons why we should be concerned about the survival and flourishing of future generations. This, it may seem, stops well short of offering us detailed guidance, or indeed any guidance, about how we should take considerations about future generations into account when we are deciding how to act.

It is true that I have not proposed a master principle with the extremely wide scope of Parfit's "Theory X," which, as we saw, is supposed to have acceptable implications when applied to all the choices people ever make. As I explained in Chapter One, I do not believe that we should allow the quest for such a principle to dictate the form that our thinking about future generations should take. Yet it is not true that my conclusions provide no normative guidance at all. I have maintained that we have strong reasons of at least four different kinds to want the chain of human generations to continue into the indefinite future under conditions conducive to human flourishing. Our reasons to want these things are also reasons to try to secure them: to do what we can, granted our limited knowledge and the fact that we face great uncertainty of many different sorts, to ensure that future generations will survive for the indefinite future and will be able to live in reasonably favorable circumstances.

This does not amount to a comprehensive principle of right action or to a precise formula that provides determinate guidance in every case. But it articulates a regulative ideal that draws on values of a number of different kinds and sets a standard of adequacy or sufficiency with clear normative significance. To say that the standard has normative significance is to say that we can violate it and that we can recognize violations of it. And we do violate it when, for example, we engage in patterns of activity that threaten to render the Earth uninhabitable for human beings by the end of this century or the next one. To my mind, the fact that such activity violates this standard provides a compelling explanation of what is objectionable about it, and it is an explanation that is not dependent on a successful conclusion to the search for a satisfactory principle of beneficence or for Parfit's "Theory X."

Nor is this explanation dependent on a highly moralized understanding of ourselves or our place in the world. The standard I have articulated is supported not, in the first instance, by an argument from moral duty or obligation but by reasons of love, interest, valuation, and reciprocity. These reasons speak to a diverse and widely shared array of human motivations. It is not only the morally heroic or the morally fastidious or the morally sensitive who have reasons to concern themselves with the fate of future generations or who can be expected, under the right conditions, to be motivated by the reasons that speak in favor of such concern.

The practical significance of this fact is evident. But it also bears on the issues that I raised at the beginning of Chapter One. My starting point was the observation that most of us lack a rich set of evaluative resources for thinking about the value of human continuity. We don't have a confident and normatively articulate understanding of our place in time or of the significance of our relations to people living at other times. The considerations I have been rehearsing in Chapters Two and Three do not contradict these observations. But they do help to explain why many people experience the poverty of our evaluative thought about the future as a form of privation and why they have an inchoate sense that other generations matter to us in ways that we can't easily explain.

Of course, the considerations I've been discussing do not by themselves remedy the deficiencies in our evaluative thought to which I have called attention. They do not supply us with a fully developed repertoire of ideas about the significance of our place in the succession of generations. No mere work of philosophy could do that. Such ideas would instead have to emerge from and be supported by much wider tendencies of thought in our culture. Who knows whether that will happen? What I have been trying to do is something much more modest. I have tried to show that we should not take our apparent temporal parochialism at face value. We should not suppose that we lack any impulse to find evaluative significance in our relations to our ancestors and descendants or that we are simply indifferent to the fate of future generations. Even in the absence of a shared understanding of the evaluative significance of our place in time, and despite our depressing record of inaction in the face of climate change and other grave threats to human survival, the structure of our own values, when considered carefully, turns out to presuppose the importance to us of human continuity and of the persistence of human generations into the future.

Whatever the potential practical significance of this fact may be, it also has implications for our understanding of ourselves and our values. It means that if we want to think further about the importance to us of our place in the chain of generations, the starting point of such reflection—the default setting from which we begin—should not be the assumption of indifference. We *already* care about our place in time and about the survival of future generations. We just need to allow ourselves to acknowledge that this is so, and then we need to do our best to draw the appropriate practical conclusions.

CHAPTER FOUR

Attachment and Axiology

I have maintained that we have reasons of at least four different kinds for caring about the fate of future generations: reasons of love, reasons of interest, reasons of valuation, and reasons of reciprocity. All these reasons depend, directly or indirectly, on what we now value, or, to put it another way, on our existing evaluative attachments. They are all, we might say, *attachment-based reasons*. This is easiest to see in the case of what I have called "reasons of valuation." These are reasons to care about the fate of future generations because the survival of so much of what we value depends on it. The dependency of these reasons on our existing evaluative attachments seems straightforward. But a similar dependency is evident with respect to reasons of love, which derive from our love of humanity, for the love of humanity is just an instance of a particular evaluative attachment: an attachment to humanity itself. And insofar as reasons of interest and reasons of reciprocity depend on our love of humanity and our existing evaluative attachments, they too depend on what we value. They too are attachment-based reasons.

The fact that our reasons for caring about the fate of future generations depend on what we now value is significant in a number of different ways. But what exactly is the nature of this dependency? In what way do our reasons depend on the fact that we value certain things? If we valued something worthless or evil, would the fact that we valued it mean that we had reasons to sustain or preserve it? Valuing something, in my view, involves a complex syndrome of attitudes and dispositions, including a belief that the thing is valuable, a susceptibility to experience a variety of context-dependent emotions concerning the thing, and a disposition to treat considerations pertaining to the thing as providing one with reasons for action in relevant deliberative contexts.[1] (Here I am using "thing" in a broad sense that encompasses any object of our valuing attitudes.) This means that it is possible to regard something as valuable without actually valuing it oneself. Indeed, most of us regard many things as valuable that we ourselves do not value. Valuing something involves more than just believing that it is valuable. Using the terminology I have introduced, we can say that it involves, in addition, a kind of *attachment to* or, alternatively, a kind of *investment in* or *engagement with* that thing. This sort of attachment or investment or engagement is constituted by the other elements of the syndrome of attitudes I have mentioned. That is, it is constituted both by emotional vulnerability and by a disposition to see oneself as having reasons for action with respect to the valued item that one does not have with respect to other comparably valuable items of the same kind.[2]

---

[1] This view is elaborated more fully in my essay "Valuing" (in *Equality and Tradition* [New York: Oxford University Press, 2010], pp. 15–40).

[2] It would be interesting and perhaps fruitful to explore possible connections between the role I ascribe to attachment, here and in the remainder of this book, and psychological "attachment theory," as developed by John Bowlby, Mary Ainsworth, and others. See, for example, Bowlby's authoritative three-volume work *Attachment and Loss* (New York: Basic Books).

If I value my relationship with you, for example, then I will typically be vulnerable to feelings of distress if you are harmed, and I will see myself as having reasons for acting in your behalf, in relevant deliberative contexts, that I do not have for acting in behalf of other equally valuable people. And so too, *mutatis mutandis*, if I value a personal project or a family heirloom. Although the specific reasons I will see myself as having will vary depending on the type of the thing that is valued, they will almost always include reasons to preserve and sustain the valued item. That is why, as I said in Chapter Three, there is a conservative dimension to valuing, something approaching a conceptual connection between valuing something and wanting it to be sustained and to persist over time. A conservative disposition to preserve and sustain the things that we value is built into our valuing attitudes.

Of course, the mere fact that we value something does not mean that we are correct to do so. We may instead be making a mistake. Usually when this happens, it is because the thing that we value lacks the value that we think it has. In addition, however, some undeniably valuable things can reasonably be valued, or can reasonably be valued in a certain way, only by people who occupy an appropriate position in relation to those things.[3] For example, in the absence of some special explanation, I cannot reasonably value your friendships in the way that you can, although I can certainly recognize their value. If I do value them in a way that is reasonable only for someone in your position, then I am making a mistake, although such cases are presumably rare and some may wonder

---

[3] For discussion, see "Valuing," pp. 36–7. One's "way" of valuing a thing, as I am understanding it, is defined by the pattern of emotional vulnerability one displays with respect to the thing and by the content and extent of the role that it plays in one's deliberations.

whether they are really possible. For present purposes, it is enough to say that, when we are mistaken in either of the two ways I have mentioned, then we do not have the reasons for action that we take ourselves to have. But in the absence of radical skepticism about value, there is no reason to think that our valuing attitudes are systematically misguided or unreasonable or that we are systematically mistaken about the content of our reasons for action. Many things are in fact valuable, and insofar as something that we value (and are in a position to value) really is valuable, we are correct in thinking that we have distinctive reasons for action with regard to that thing. These reasons are over and above any reasons that we and others may have solely in virtue of the intrinsic value of the thing.

So, to return to my earlier example, if I value my friendship with you, and if our friendship is indeed valuable, then I am correct in thinking that I have reasons to act in your behalf that other people do not have and that I do not have with regard to people who are not my friends. And if I value an antique rug that has been in my family for generations, and if the rug really is valuable, then I am correct in thinking that I have reasons to care for it or preserve it that other people do not have and that I do not have with regard to other valuable antique rugs. This does not mean that I have no reason to do anything at all in behalf of people who are not my friends, or, indeed, that I never have reasons to help preserve other antique rugs or other people's family heirlooms. It means only that, by virtue of valuing particular valuable things (that we are in a position to value), we have reasons for action that go beyond the reasons that we and others may have solely in virtue of the intrinsic value of those things.

If what I have been saying is correct, then the mere fact that we value something is not by itself sufficient for us to have such reasons. In addition, the things that we value must themselves be valuable, and we must be in an appropriate position to value them. These conditions together are sufficient. For the purposes of this discussion, the important point is that the four types of attachment-based reason that we have for caring about the fate of future generations all satisfy these conditions. Although they depend on our existing values and evaluative attachments, and go beyond any reasons that derive solely from the intrinsic value of the things to which we are attached, they are genuine reasons only because and only insofar as (a) the things that we value are in fact valuable and (b) we occupy a position that makes sense of our valuing those things.

Since attachment-based reasons depend on our valuing attitudes, and since a conservative disposition is built into those attitudes, such reasons depend on and reflect our conservative disposition. Yet the idea that our reasons for caring about the fate of future generations depend on an essentially conservative disposition may seem surprising.[4] In this chapter and the one that follows, I want to examine the role of the conservative disposition further, with the aim of illuminating three different topics. The first topic, which I will discuss in this chapter and to which I will return at the end of the next one, is the contrast between this understanding of our concern for future generations and an alternative understanding that is suggested by the beneficence-based approach to population ethics. The second topic is the conservative disposition itself: what exactly it consists in, how it is best understood, and how it is distinguished from other forms of conservatism. The final topic is how to situate the conservative disposition so understood in the context of the more

---

[4] But for a qualified defense of a similar idea, see Torbjörn Tännsjö, *Conservatism for Our Time* (London: Routledge, 1990), especially chapter 5 ("A Conservative Argument for the Preservation of the Human Species").

general relations between our valuing attitudes and our attitudes toward time. I will discuss these last two topics in Chapter Five.

One lesson of the argument I have been developing is that, with respect to value at least, there is a sense in which the present depends on the future. Without confidence in the survival of humanity into the future, our ability to find value in our activities here and now would be eroded. The most obvious source of resistance to this idea lies in the fact that most of us are not aware of attaching anything like this kind of value or importance to the survival of future generations. Most of the time, we don't think much about the question of humanity's survival one way or the other. Most of us are far more preoccupied with the activities we are engaged in here and now, with the struggles of daily existence, and with the values that we hope to realize in our own lives. The suggestion that, despite this, we care so much about the survival of humanity that our ability to find value in our daily lives depends on our confidence that human beings will survive may seem mysterious or incredible.

The role of the conservative disposition in supporting a concern with the fate of future generations helps to dispel the mystery. Although, as I have maintained, our ability to find value in our present activities depends on assumptions we make about the future, it is also true that our evaluative attitudes toward the future depend, via our conservative disposition, on the values we affirm in the present. Our reasons for concerning ourselves with humanity's survival in the future are rooted in our present-day love of humanity and our existing attachments to all of the many things we now value that consist in or depend on forms of human activity. And it is because we care about humanity's survival in the future that the prospect of its extinction would compromise our capacity to find value in our activities here and now. This means that there is a virtuous circle that ties together our attitudes toward time and value now and in the future. The values that we now accept give us strong reasons to care about the future of humanity, and in fact we do care about it, so much so that the prospect of human extinction would compromise our ability to find value in our present activities.

The relationship I have sketched between our conservative disposition and our concern for future generations gives rise to a number of questions. As I have said, it raises questions about the nature of the relevant kind of conservatism and about the unity of our diverse attitudes toward time and value. But before addressing those questions, I want to contrast this way of understanding the sources of our concern about humanity's future with an alternative understanding that is suggested by the beneficence-based approach to future generations.

One naïve but natural thought is that a concern for future generations is a purely forward-looking attitude and that conservatism is a purely backward-looking disposition, so that either the two have nothing to do with each other or else there is a conflict between them. Conservatives, it may seem, want to preserve the status quo, whereas those who take seriously our responsibilities toward future generations want to change or reorient it. According to the attachment-based view I have been setting out, however, a concern for the future of humanity flows naturally from, and is given rational and motivational support by, a conservative concern for the things that we value now. It is our existing evaluative attachments that propel our concerns into the future.

Things look very different from the perspective of the beneficence-based literature on future generations. The primary focus of that literature is on questions of "population ethics," and one of the standard methods that is used to investigate those questions is to describe alternative worlds, or alternative states of a particular world, whose populations differ from one another in their size, composition, and/or levels of well-being, and then to compare the value of those worlds or states. The hope is that by collecting our judgments about many such cases, we can arrive at a satisfactory "population axiology"—a principle or standard that would allow us systematically to assess the relative value of total states of the world when their populations differ in one or more of the respects I have mentioned. In the representative formulation of Hilary Greaves, "A population axiology is a betterness ordering of states of affairs, where the states of affairs include ones in which different numbers of persons are ever born."[5] A satisfactory population axiology, if one could be identified, would in turn supply the basis for a principle of beneficence, which would spell out, either by itself or in conjunction with some other principles, our responsibilities for promoting the best available population outcomes.

There is no consensus among those who hope to find a satisfactory population axiology about which one is the best candidate.[6] But even if there were such a consensus, what kind of authority is the preferred axiology supposed to have? Why is it thought either that we do or that we should care which population outcomes are

---

[5] Hilary Greaves, "Population Axiology," *Philosophy Compass* 12(11), 1–15 at 1.

[6] Thus Greaves (ibid.), who says that "any plausible theory of population ethics" must include a population axiology, also says that "every extant population axiology is open to serious objection" (pp. 1, 12). Furthermore, some theorists have presented formal proofs of various impossibility theorems, which purport to demonstrate that no population axiology can simultaneously satisfy each of a small number of intuitively compelling constraints. See, for example, Gustaf Arrhenius, "An Impossibility Theorem for Welfarist Axiologies," *Economics and Philosophy* 16(2000): 247–66.

judged superior by the lights of this or that axiological principle? For many axiologists, the importance of bringing about whatever population outcomes are best derives simply from the fact that they *are* best, in a sense which implies that we have *pro tanto* reasons to bring them about if we can.[7] On this view, there is a sense in which the authority of population axiology over our reasons and motives derives from nothing other than population axiology itself. We have impersonal reasons to make the world go as well as it can go; in particular, we have impersonal reasons to bring about the best population outcomes we can achieve, whatever those outcomes may be. And in order to determine which outcomes are best, we have no alternative but to engage in direct axiological argument: direct argument, for example, about the relative value of states of the world that differ in the size and/or levels of well-being of their populations.

My aim in this chapter is not to criticize the axiological approach to questions about future generations but rather to elucidate the contrast between that approach and the attachment-based approach that I have been developing in this book. The axiological approach, at least when interpreted along the lines I have been discussing, treats the existence and well-being of human beings—or, perhaps, the existence of what Larry Temkin calls "high-quality life"[8] more generally—as great impersonal values which we have strong reasons to promote. It would simply be a *bad thing*—indeed, Parfit says it would be "*much* worse than most people think"[9]—if humankind

---

[7] On the "reason-implying sense" of "good" and its cognates, see Parfit, *On What Matters* (Oxford: Oxford University Press, 2011), chapter 1.

[8] Temkin, "Rationality with Respect to People, Places, and Times," *Canadian Journal of Philosophy* 45(2016): 576–608.

[9] Parfit, *Reasons and Persons* (Oxford: Clarendon Press, 1984), p. 453.

(and other forms of "high-quality life") were to disappear from the universe forever. According to the attachment-based perspective that I have been defending, by contrast, we have a variety of reasons, which are rooted in our existing attachments to humanity and to valued forms of human activity and endeavor, to care about the capacity of future generations to survive and to flourish. What those reasons support is not a generic concern for the promotion or realization of impersonal value, but rather a more specific desire, rooted in the values we affirm in our daily lives, that the chain of generations should be extended into the indefinite future and that our successors should be able to live under conditions conducive to their flourishing. From this perspective, it would be a mistake to think that our reasons for caring about the fate of future generations are hostage to our ability to construct a satisfactory population axiology, a satisfactory theory of the relative goodness of total states of the world that differ only in relevant population-related respects.

Yet, despite these disclaimers, my account of our attachment-based reasons for wanting future generations to survive and to flourish may seem implicitly to presuppose such an axiology. After all, I said at the beginning of this chapter that attachment-based reasons are genuine reasons only insofar as the things to which we are attached are in fact valuable. And I have been taking it for granted that, insofar as those things are valuable, everyone has at least some reasons for treating them in certain ways in virtue of their value. That is, everyone has reasons for undertaking or refraining from undertaking certain actions with respect to them. If this is correct, then it follows that our attachment-based reasons presuppose other, *attachment-independent* reasons that apply to everyone. To be sure, the content and extent of these reasons may not be easy to specify and is likely to vary from case to case. And, as we have seen, those who value a particular valuable thing normally have reasons that go far beyond any reasons that those who do not value the thing may have. Still, our attachment-independent reasons may be very significant. Insofar as a valuable thing is liable to damage or destruction, for example, it seems plausible to say that, at the very least, everyone has an attachment-independent reason not to damage or destroy it without compelling reason to do so.

The relevance of this fact for questions about future generations is evident. It implies, for example, that our attachment-based reasons of love are genuine reasons only if humanity, which is the object of our love, is in fact valuable. And if humanity is in fact valuable, then even those who do not exhibit a love of humanity nevertheless have, at a minimum, attachment-independent reasons not to damage or destroy it. Similarly, it implies that our attachment-based reasons of valuation are genuine reasons only if the things that we value are in fact valuable. And if those things are in fact valuable, then, again, even people who do not value them have attachment-independent reasons not to damage or destroy them.

If this is right, then, in addition to the four types of attachment-based reason I have discussed, we must recognize a broad class of attachment-independent reasons for concerning ourselves with the fate of humanity. We can call these *reasons of value*, to distinguish them from the attachment-based *reasons of valuation* that I have already discussed. Reasons of value depend not on our love of humanity but solely on humanity's value, and not on our attachments to the many valuable things that consist in or depend on forms of human activity, but solely on the value of those things themselves.

Although this is an important conclusion, it is not by itself enough to motivate the enterprise of population axiology as I have been understanding it. That is, it does not show that we need a general, reason-implying theory of the relative goodness of total states of the world that differ only in population-related respects. Nor does it show that an attachment-based view requires such an axiology. To see why not, consider first a frivolous analogy. The attachment-based reasons of valuation that one has in virtue of one's love of baseball may presuppose that baseball is valuable, and the fact that it is valuable may mean that everyone has at least some attachment-independent reasons of value relating to baseball. Perhaps, for example, everyone has *pro tanto* reasons to avoid disrupting games of baseball, to respect the desires of some people to play baseball and of other people to watch baseball being played, and to refrain from disparaging people when they do these things. However, even if baseball is valuable, it hardly follows that everyone has *pro tanto* reasons to try to bring about states of the world that are optimal in baseball-related respects. Indeed, it does not follow that there *are* states of the world that are "optimal in baseball-related respects." That is, it does not follow that we need, or should in principle expect to find, an axiological principle that would enable us to assess the relative value of alternative worlds, or alternative total states of a particular world, which differ only in the number of baseball games played, the quality of those games, and their temporal and geographical distribution. Still less does this follow if we assume that such a principle would have to support the claim that everyone has *pro tanto* reasons, even if very weak *pro tanto* reasons, to try to bring about the best possible baseball-related states of our world. Not only do these things not follow, but nobody is tempted to think in these terms. Even if we are fully responsive to the value of baseball, there is no intellectual or practical pressure to develop a baseball axiology.[10]

---

[10] Those who are not baseball-lovers may object that this analogy is not merely frivolous but misleading. Baseball is not really valuable, they

Consider now a less frivolous example. The attachment-based reasons of valuation that one has in virtue of the importance one assigns to friendship may presuppose that friendship is valuable, and the fact that it is valuable may mean that everyone has at least some attachment-independent reasons of value relating to friendship. But it does not follow from the fact that friendship is valuable that we need or should expect to find a friendship axiology: a principle that would enable us (a) to assess the relative value of total states of the world that differ only in the number, quality, and distribution of friendships within them, and (b) to assert that everyone has *pro tanto* reasons to try to bring about the best friendship-related states of the world that they can. All that follows from the fact that friendship is valuable is that we should be suitably responsive to that value, not that we should expect to find a reason-implying friendship axiology. As in the case of baseball, there is no intellectual or practical pressure to think in these terms, and nobody actually does so.[11]

I believe that what applies to baseball and friendship also applies to our attachment-based reasons for wanting future generations of human beings to survive and to flourish. One can acknowledge that, in general, our attachments are reason-giving only if the objects of those attachments are valuable independently of our being attached to them, and that this is no less true of an attachment to humanity than it is of any of our other attachments. One

---

may say, and that is why we shouldn't expect to find a baseball axiology. But exactly the same points would hold if one substituted for the love of baseball a love of poetry or music or Shakespeare's plays or any one of countless other practices or creative products or pursuits.

[11] For related remarks about friendship, see T.M. Scanlon, *What We Owe to Each Other* (Cambridge, MA: Harvard University Press, 1998), pp. 88–90.

can also acknowledge that, in consequence, all people have at least some attachment-independent reasons with respect to humanity, whether or not they exhibit the distinctive form of attachment that I am calling a love of humanity. Yet it does not follow from these acknowledgements that one is committed to the existence of a population axiology: a reason-implying betterness ordering of total states of the world that differ only in relevant population-related respects. There is no automatic step from the value of humanity to the need for such an axiology. If there is pressure to develop one, it must have an independent source.

A related point applies to the idea of beneficence. As I have said, our love of humanity gives us attachment-based "reasons of love" only if humanity is valuable independently of our attachment to it. And if humanity is valuable independently of our attachment to it, then everyone has attachment-independent reasons of value with respect to human life and human flourishing. It does not seem inappropriate to characterize this subset of reasons of value as *reasons of beneficence*. It follows that, on my view, some people have reasons of love only if all people have reasons of beneficence. This means that, despite the reservations I have expressed about beneficence-based approaches to issues concerning future generations, my view is committed both to recognizing beneficence as an important value in general and to accepting that we have beneficence-based reasons for concern about future generations in particular.

As with other attachment-independent reasons of value, however, both the content and the extent of these reasons of beneficence remain open and require investigation. The recognition of these reasons does not by itself settle the question, which I raised in Chapter One, of how, in general, the content of beneficence is best understood. It does not vindicate the idea of a utilitarian-style "principle of beneficence" that relies on some axiological theory nor does it rule out alternative, non-utilitarian interpretations of beneficence as a value. Nor, with respect to future generations in particular, does it tell us exactly what the content of our reasons of beneficence is.

One suggestion might be that, as applied to questions about future generations, reasons of beneficence consist solely in reasons not to damage or destroy humanity, and that there are no attachment-independent reasons to take affirmative steps to sustain and preserve future generations. In general, as we've seen, those who value a valuable thing normally have reasons for treating that thing in certain ways that go far beyond any reasons that those who do not value the thing may have. For example, my attachment-independent reasons to treat (and to avoid treating) your friends and your family heirlooms in certain ways are undoubtedly significant, but they appear to be largely negative in character. I should not abuse your friends or damage or destroy your heirlooms, but your reasons, which include attachment-based reasons for treating your friends and family heirlooms in certain ways, are much more far-reaching. They are not limited to reasons to avoid abuse or mistreatment, but instead support a much richer and more varied array of actions. Similarly, we might surmise that, with respect to future generations, those who exhibit a love of humanity have attachment-based reasons of love that go far beyond the exclusively attachment-independent reasons possessed by those who exhibit no love of humanity. Perhaps our attachment-independent reasons of beneficence are limited to "negative" reasons to avoid damaging or destroying human life, and only our attachment-based reasons include "positive" reasons to help sustain humanity. We can call this "the limited interpretation" of beneficence.

In the context of concerns about climate change, nuclear proliferation, and other threats to the future of humanity, even purely negative reasons to avoid damaging or destroying human life would, as I have said, have important practical implications. However, insofar as it construes our attachment-independent reasons of beneficence as having an exclusively negative character, the limited interpretation is too restrictive. To see why, we may first observe that, contrary to our initial speculation, such an interpretation would also be too restrictive if applied to our other attachment-independent reasons. Appearances to the contrary notwithstanding, the attachment-independent reasons that I have with respect to your friends and family heirlooms are not, in fact, exclusively negative in character. Under some conditions, I may well have "positive" reasons to help your friends and to save your heirlooms from destruction. And since the value of humanity is very great, our attachment-independent reasons of beneficence may be correspondingly more far-reaching.

Nevertheless, it does not follow that these reasons must take the form of reasons to maximize human well-being or to maximize the numbers of people who can lead good lives or to promote optimal population outcomes as picked out by some axiological principle. Insofar as they bear on questions about future generations, they may instead be reasons whose content is no different from the content of our attachment-based reasons. That is, they may be reasons to ensure that the chain of human generations is extended into the indefinite future under conditions conducive to human flourishing. Where future generations are concerned, in other words, the content of our attachment-independent reasons of beneficence may be identical to the content of our attachment-based reasons, despite the fact that they have a different source.

The important point is this. From the fact that our reasons of beneficence have an attachment-independent source, it does not follow that their content must be understood along utilitarian or axiological lines. It does not follow even if we assume that, with respect to the future of humanity, our reasons of beneficence are more extensive than the limited interpretation would allow. If there is some reason to conceive of these reasons in utilitarian or axiological terms, it must come from somewhere else. There is no direct route from the bare fact that humanity is valuable to a conception of beneficence as requiring us, *ceteris paribus*, to promote optimal population outcomes. The content of beneficence depends not merely on the fact that humanity is valuable but, just as importantly, on how we have reason to respond to its value.[12] And to me, at least, it is far less plausible that we have reason to respond to humanity's value by trying to promote optimal population outcomes than that we have reason to respond by trying to ensure that the chain of human generations is extended into the indefinite future under conditions conducive to human flourishing. After all, if even a love of humanity does not give us a general, context-independent reason to promote optimal population outcomes, it is far from clear why the value of humanity alone should do so. Of course, some will disagree. Still, the fact remains that one cannot derive a utilitarian or axiological interpretation of beneficence simply from the premise that humanity is valuable, for there are other interpretations of beneficence that are compatible with that premise.

My aims in this chapter have been twofold. First, I have tried to make clear the contrast between an axiological approach to questions about future generations and my own approach, which is

[12] Johann Frick makes a related claim in his paper "On the Survival of Humanity," *Canadian Journal of Philosophy* 47(2017): 344–67. Frick argues that our reasons to care about future generations should be conceptualized, not in the way that utilitarians and other consequentialists do, but rather as reasons to cherish and preserve humanity which are grounded in humanity's "final value."

predominantly attachment-based, but which, as I have said, also recognizes some attachment-independent reasons for concerning ourselves with the fate of our successors. Second, I have tried to show that the recognition of attachment-independent reasons of value does not commit us to the quest for a satisfactory population axiology or to the search for a principle of beneficence that depends on such an axiology.

My aim in Chapter Five will be to develop further the alternative, predominantly attachment-based perspective that I have been outlining. We can think of that perspective as having both normative and motivational dimensions. Normatively, there is a set of reasons, whether moral or non-moral, to secure the ability of our successors to survive under conditions conducive to their flourishing. Motivationally, there is a conservative disposition to sustain the humanity we love and the existing values we affirm. Having concentrated in the previous chapters primarily on the normative dimension of this perspective, I want next to explore its motivational side. At the motivational level, the fact that it grounds our concern for future generations in a conservative disposition to sustain our existing attachments puts that concern on a secure footing and integrates it into a unified stance we may take toward the diachronic dimension of our values. Or so I will argue in Chapter Five. I will begin by trying to clarify the kind of conservatism on which this perspective relies.

CHAPTER FIVE
Conservatism, Temporal Bias, and Future Generations

The conservative disposition

The conservative disposition to which I have referred in previous chapters is not a form of political conservatism. It is a disposition to preserve or sustain the things that we value, and both the things that we value and the steps necessary to preserve them may conflict sharply with the policies and practices endorsed by political conservatives. One way to illuminate this kind of value conservatism is to consider how it relates to the form of conservatism defended by G.A. Cohen, with which it has much in common.

In his wonderful essay defending what he calls "small-c conservatism," Cohen advocates a "bias in favor of existing value" (p. 210), by which he means that we should regret the destruction of particular valuable things as such, even when it would lead to their replacement by things of greater value.[1,2] He thinks that "everyone who is sane" (p. 204) has this bias to some degree, and that it is "rational and right" (p. 210) that they should. For Cohen, the crucial distinction is between value in the abstract and the particular things that have value, or, alternatively, between the value that things bear and the bearers of such value. The conservatism that he defends holds that particular things that have value take priority over value itself, in at least two related senses. First, particular valuable things do not matter or count simply because of the amount of value that they bear or that "resides in them" (p. 206). Second, we have at least some (defeasible) reason to preserve particular valuable things as such, even if by sacrificing them we could produce more value

---

[1] G.A. Cohen, "Rescuing Conservatism: A Defense of Existing Value," in R.J. Wallace, R. Kumar, and S. Freeman, eds., *Reasons and Recognition: Essays on the Philosophy of T.M. Scanlon* (New York: Oxford University Press, 2011), pp. 203–30, at 210. Hereafter, page references to this article will be given parenthetically in the text. An alternative version of the article (the "All Souls version") is included as Chapter 8 in *Finding Oneself in the Other* (Princeton, NJ: Princeton University Press, 2012), a posthumous collection of Cohen's essays edited by Michael Otsuka. The differences between the two versions of the essay are explained by Otsuka in his Preface to the volume and do not affect my discussion of Cohen's position.

[2] Cohen distinguishes between *particular value* and *personal value* as sources of conservative attitudes. For him, particular value is something that an item has *as* the particular item it is, whereas personal value is something that an item has because of its relation to some person. My initial summary of his view in the opening text of this section concentrates on what he says about particular value and sets aside his remarks about personal value, both because they are much briefer and because I find them obscure in certain respects. However, I discuss the relation between his two categories of value in greater detail in footnote 9 below.

overall. The upshot is that particular valuable things command a kind of loyalty. They do not become dispensable the minute we could replace them with something of greater value. Conservatives of Cohen's sort will be (defeasibly) disposed to retain particular valuable things even if it means forgoing the opportunity to make things in general as valuable as possible.[3]

Cohen too insists that the conservatism he defends is not political Conservatism (or what he calls "big-C Conservatism") as it is understood in the United Kingdom or the United States. For one thing, what he favors is the conservation of intrinsic value, and since injustice and exploitation lack such value, there is no case for conserving them. To the extent that the policies endorsed by political conservatives are unjust, then, Cohen's form of conservatism provides no basis for defending them. Of course, something that is unjust may nevertheless be valuable in other respects, and although it would be possible to give justice lexical priority over the conservation of value, Cohen is not sure he is willing to go that far. Yet he

---

[3] In the course of trying to develop an adequate theodicy, Robert Adams expresses an attitude that seems congenial to Cohen's conservatism and relates it directly to questions about future generations. Adams writes: "I would quite strongly prefer the preservation of the human race, for example, to its ultimate replacement by a more excellent species, and think none the worse of myself for the preference. Similarly I think it may be a good thing, and no sign of imperfection, for someone to favor the preservation and internal development of a particular civilization (e.g. Chinese or Western) or national culture (e.g. Welsh) though he knows that such a continuation will occupy space and resources from which something even more excellent could grow instead. A good person accepts significant costs—and sometimes, where he has a right to, imposes them on others—for the sake of what he loves, and not only for the sake of what is best" ("Existence, Self-Interest, and the Problem of Evil," *Noûs* 13[1979]: 53–65, at 62).

indicates that he is much less willing than big-C Conservatives to tolerate unjust social arrangements for the sake of the other values they may realize or facilitate. In addition, Cohen argues that the economic market is hostile to conservatism in his sense, since it is always prepared to trade a valuable particular for something that has more value. So free-market Conservatism is deeply anti-conservative in his sense. Under capitalism, he says, the British Conservative Party turned into the "anti-conservative market party." As he puts it in an especially memorable passage: "For the sake of protecting and extending the powers of wealth, big-C Conservatives regularly sacrifice the small c-conservatism that many of them genuinely cherish. They blather on (as Prime Minister John Major did) about warm beer and sturdy spinsters cycling to church and then they hand Wal-Mart the keys to the kingdom. They are thereby in tune with the propensity of capitalism, which is to maximize a certain kind of value, in sovereign disregard of the value of any *things*" (p. 225).[4]

Cohen contrasts his view not only with free-market Conservatism but also with normative ethical theories like utilitarianism that favor the maximization of value. "To seek to maximize value," he writes, "is to see nothing wrong in the destruction of valuable things, as long as there is no reduction in the total amount of value as a result. Unlike the conservative, the utilitarian is indifferent

---

[4] In referring to John Major, Cohen presumably had in mind the following passage from a speech Major gave as Prime Minister to the Conservative Group for Europe on April 22, 1993: "Fifty years from now Britain will still be the country of long shadows on county grounds, warm beer, invincible green suburbs, dog lovers and pools fillers and—as George Orwell said—'old maids bicycling to Holy Communion through the morning mist' and if we get our way—Shakespeare still read even in school. Britain will survive unamendable in all essentials." Text available at www.johnmajor.co.uk/page1086.html.

between adding to what we have now got, at no cost, something that has five units of value, and adding something worth ten units of value at the expense of destroying something worth five. The utilitarian says: 'Let us have as much value as possible, regardless of what happens, as a result of that policy, to existing bearers of value: they do not matter, *as such*.' Conservatism sets itself against that maximizing attitude, according to which the things that possess value, by contrast with the value they possess, do not matter at all" (pp. 211–12).

One can imagine a utilitarian complaining that this is a distortion. Utilitarianism does not endorse the sacrifice of existing valuable things for the sake of value in the abstract. The sacrifices or trade-offs it favors will always involve exchanging some valuable things for other valuable things, either ones that already exist or ones that will come to exist in the future. When value is maximized, in other words, that value will always reside in particular bearers of value. Value is not, so to speak, free-floating. So it is misleading to represent utilitarianism as sacrificing particular valuable things for the sake of "value *itself*" (p. 210).

Cohen would presumably be unmoved by this complaint. If the utilitarian is willing to sacrifice a particular valuable thing whenever it can be replaced by another particular thing with even slightly more value, then the original item is being valued solely in proportion to the value that it bears. And to say that just is to say that the utilitarian, unlike the conservative, does not value the bearers of value independently of the value that they bear.

Yet Cohen concedes, in response to a point made by Michael Otsuka, that his form of conservatism does not exclude all forms of value-maximization. Although it rules out "comprehensive" value-maximization, it allows for "local" maximization, in which one valuable existing thing is sacrificed in order to save a greater number of equally valuable existing things, thus maximizing the quantity of "preserved value." This naturally invites questions of two different kinds. The first is why a willingness to maximize the quantity of preserved value, unlike a willingness to maximize the quantity of value *simpliciter*, does not amount to giving the value that things have priority over the things themselves. The second question is whether, once the door is opened to local value-maximization, it is possible to block all forms of comprehensive value-maximization. For example, would Cohen's conservatism rule out a comprehensive value-maximizing form of consequentialism that treated the maximization of preserved value as lexically prior to the maximization of newly created value?

These are not questions I plan to pursue here. Instead, I want to make a different observation about the structure of Cohen's position. Cohen's conservatism appears to combine two things: an assignment of priority to the bearers of value over the value that they bear, and an assignment of priority to those particular bearers of value that already exist over those particular bearers of value that do not yet exist. Cohen does not always distinguish sharply between these two forms of priority. Without the second form, however, there is nothing distinctively conservative about his position. It is only the second form of priority that may be said to constitute a bias in favor of existing value. But although Cohen offers arguments that support the first form of priority, he never actually defends the second form, nor is it clear how he would want to do so.

To see both of these points more clearly, consider the position of someone I'll call *Jill*, who is a painter. Jill is not, let us suppose, a utilitarian, or indeed a consequentialist of any sort, nor is she much disposed to engage in philosophical reflection about value. She simply wants to paint, which is to say she wants to create paintings, and of course she wants them to be good paintings. This means, in

Cohen's terminology, that she wants to create particular valuable things. She certainly does not want to create value in the abstract. In saying this, I am not just making the pedantic point that one can paint only paintings—that there's no such thing as painting value in the abstract. My point, instead, is this. Even if Jill knew that, by abandoning her own career as a painter, she could earn enough money to fully fund the careers of two painters even more talented than herself, she would decline. In this sense, she wants to create particular valuable paintings, rather than to maximize the creation of artistic value or even to maximize the creation of particular valuable paintings. Rather than becoming a painter, moreover, Jill could have devoted herself to the preservation of existing valuable things— she could, for example, have become an art conservator—but she has chosen instead to create new valuable things. And, we may suppose, she would have made the same choice even if she knew that she would be able to paint only n new paintings over the course of her career, while as a conservator she would have been able to preserve $n+1$ existing paintings.

What are we to say about Jill? On the one hand, she respects the priority of particular valuable things over value in the abstract. Her aim is to create particular valuable paintings, not to maximize artistic value. On the other hand, she does not, in deciding how to live, give priority to those valuable things that already exist over those that do not yet exist. If she did, she would have chosen to become an art conservator rather than a painter. So, it seems, she is not a conservative in Cohen's sense, but neither does she make the mistake about value that he believes non-conservatives make. But if one can avoid that mistake without being a conservative, it follows that Cohen has given no argument for conservatism per se. Nor has he given any argument for a bias in favor of existing value. He has simply given an argument for assigning particular valuable things priority over value in the abstract, and, as Jill's example demonstrates, one need not be a conservative to do that.

Cohen more or less concedes this point in response to an objection along similar lines that he attributes to Anca Gheaus. He responds to Gheaus as follows:

> If Gheaus is right, my defense of what I call conservatism is not impeached, but that which I defend is now seen to be an instance of something more general, namely of the claims of particular valuable things over value in general. So, for example, we see the bias in valuing particular things over abstract value in the typical (not universal, to be sure) aspiration of the artist, who is aiming not to produce a certain mass or type of value but a particular valuable thing. In a post-Gheaus reworking of the theme of this essay, the emphasis on particular valuable things *that now exist* would be relaxed. (p. 220)

When Cohen says that his conservatism is not "impeached" by Gheaus's point, but merely shown to be an instance of something more general, this seems misleading. What Gheaus's point and Jill's example suggest is that there may be no more reason to conserve existing valuable things than there is to create new valuable things, so long as in each case the particular things are given priority over "value" in the abstract. In other words, Cohen's conservatism is not impeached only if it is taken to consist solely in asserting the claims of particular valuable things over value in the abstract, and to include no priority at all for those particular things that already exist over those that do not yet exist.

If that is what Cohen's position amounts to in the end, then it seems misleading to call it a form of conservatism, although it may nevertheless be correct. Perhaps the lesson to be drawn from Gheaus's point and Jill's example is that there is no reason to give those particular things that already exist priority over those that do not. The conservative bias in favor of existing value is unjustified.

I believe that this is too sweeping a conclusion, and that it is possible to locate, in the general vicinity of Cohen's argument, an important insight about the difference between our characteristic attitudes toward valuable things that already exist and our attitudes toward valuable things that do not (yet) exist. This insight provides support for the form of conservatism that I want to defend. However, the insight is best appreciated if we focus, not on *the value of particular things*, as Cohen does, but rather on what it is for a person *to value* a particular thing.[5] Although Cohen himself uses both of these locutions, the distinction between them plays no substantive role in his account. By contrast, I have already indicated that I regard the distinction between something's having value and someone's valuing the thing as very significant.[6]

As I have explained, I see valuing as involving a complex syndrome of attitudes and dispositions, including not only a belief that the thing is valuable but also a susceptibility to experience a variety of context-dependent emotions concerning the thing and a disposition to treat considerations pertaining to the thing as providing one

---

[5] For this reason, I am sympathetic to Ralf Bader's conclusion, in his review of *Finding Oneself in the Other*, that Cohen's conservatism is not best understood axiologically. Bader's review appears in *Notre Dame Philosophical Reviews* (April, 2013) and is accessible online at http://ndpr.nd.edu/news/38715-finding-oneself-in-the-other/.

[6] As I said in footnote 2 above, Cohen distinguishes between *particular value* and *personal value*. He also draws a corresponding distinction between *particular valuing* and *personal valuing*. But the distinction that matters to him is the distinction between the particular and the personal, not the distinction between value and valuing. Some (though not all) of what Cohen tries to capture with his distinction between the particular and the personal is, I believe, better captured by the distinction between value and valuing. See footnote 9 below.

with reasons for action in relevant contexts. It is not only possible but commonplace to regard something as valuable (or, in Cohen's terms, as possessing "particular value") without actually valuing it oneself in this sense. Valuing something involves, in addition to regarding it as valuable, a kind of attachment or investment or engagement that is constituted by the other elements of the syndrome of attitudes and dispositions. It is constituted by patterns of emotional vulnerability and by a disposition to see oneself as having reasons for action with respect to the valued item that one does not have with respect to other comparably valuable items of the same kind. Although the contours of these patterns of emotional engagement and the content of these reasons can vary depending on the type of thing that is in question, the emotions will in most cases include vulnerability to feelings of distress if the thing is harmed or damaged or destroyed and, as I have emphasized in previous chapters, the reasons will almost always have a conservative dimension: they will include reasons to sustain and preserve the things that we value.

These points about the relation between valuing and reasons for action are important for two reasons. First, they demonstrate that, insofar as a conservative disposition to sustain the things that we value is built into our valuing attitudes, every valuer must possess such a disposition. This is in the spirit of Cohen's assertion that "everyone who is sane has *something* of" the conservative disposition (p. 204). Second, and of special importance for present purposes, they help to explain why a conservative disposition of the kind I am defending includes a bias in favor of valuable things that already exist, and does not consist solely in a temporally neutral assignment of priority to the bearers of value over the value that they bear.

The explanation turns on the observation that we cannot, in general, value things that do not exist, and have never existed, in the way that we value existing things. Valuing involves attachment, attachment requires acquaintance, and one cannot be acquainted, in the relevant sense, with something that has never yet existed.[7] So, for example, one cannot value the friendships one has not yet formed in the way that one values one's existing friendships. One cannot value the projects one will someday develop in the way that one values the projects one already has. One cannot value the children one has not yet conceived in the way that one values one's existing children. Nor can one now value the great works of art that artists will produce in the future in the way one values those great works that already exist. One can, of course, attach value to one's prospects and plans before they have borne fruit and to one's hopes and dreams before they have been fulfilled. But in these cases the prospects and plans and hopes and dreams already exist. One cannot in the same way attach value to the plans one has not yet made or the dreams one does not yet have.

Perhaps there are unusual cases in which something that does not yet exist can nevertheless be the object of affective attitudes similar to those that are characteristic of attachment. If you know that the child you expect someday to have will inherit a congenital

---

[7] It would, of course, be desirable to provide a developed account of the relevant notion of acquaintance, but I cannot do that here. Suffice it to say that I am using the term informally and colloquially, and not in any of the more specialized senses that have featured in epistemology and the philosophy of mind since the publication of Russell's "Knowledge by Acquaintance and Knowledge by Description," *Proceedings of the Aristotelian Society* 11 (1910–11): 108–28. For relevant discussion of the ethical significance of attachment and acquaintance, see the recent series of papers by Kieran Setiya: "Retrospection," *Philosophers' Imprint* 16, No. 15 (2015), "Other People" (unpublished draft), and "Ignorance, Beneficence, and Rights" (unpublished draft).

disease from which you suffer, for example, then perhaps you can feel not just regret *about that fact* but sorrow *for the child*.[8] Yet this by itself falls short of the full-fledged syndrome of attitudes and dispositions that is characteristic of attachment. And even if one thinks that there can be cases of full-fledged attachment to future existents, one can hardly deny that such attachments are far rarer than attachments to things that already exist or that there is far less scope for establishing them. If this is correct, then it follows that the conservative disposition to sustain the things that we value goes beyond a temporally neutral assignment of priority to the bearers of value over the value that they bear. It includes, in addition, a bias in favor of particular bearers of value that already exist as compared with those that do not yet exist. The bias derives from the fact that we can form value-based attachments to existing things in a way that we cannot, in general, form such attachments to things that do not yet exist. Inasmuch as our valuing attitudes can be directed only (or primarily) at those bearers of value that already exist or have already existed, the conservative disposition I am defending recognizes special reasons for preserving and sustaining existing valuable things, and special reasons for regretting their loss or destruction. This vindicates a form of conservatism that has a great deal in common with the conservatism that Cohen endorses.[9]

[8] I owe the example to Ketan Ramakrishnan.
[9] However, because the conservative disposition as I have described it depends on *attachment*, it does not apply to those existing bearers of value to which we are not attached. If there is a case for extending the disposition to them too, as Cohen may believe there is, the explanation must be different. There is a related interpretive point. Because the conservative disposition as I have described it depends on attachment, it may seem that it would have to be situated, in terms of Cohen's classification scheme, entirely within the category of "personal" as opposed to "particular" value

At the same time, it is important not to exaggerate or misinterpret the normative significance of the conservative disposition as I have characterized it. Although we have special reasons for action pertaining to items that we already value, these reasons will not always be the strongest reasons that we have. In any given case, they may be outweighed by sufficiently strong reasons of other kinds. Furthermore, there will be many cases in which we can create new items of value without neglecting the reasons we have to care for the items we already value. That's how it was, or so we may suppose, with Jill, the painter. She did not need to neglect her reasons to care

(and valuing). Recall that for Cohen, particular value is something that an item has *as* the particular item it is, whereas personal value is something that an item has because of its relation to some person. Correspondingly, particular valuing consists in valuing an item *as* the particular item it is, whereas personal valuing consists in valuing an item because of one's special relation to it. In my terms, however, valuing always involves relational elements, and so it may seem that it would always count as "personal" in Cohen's sense. And what Cohen calls "particular valuing" does not appear to be a form of valuing in my sense at all; it is closer to simply "regarding as valuable." Yet valuing in my sense also involves, in addition to its relational elements, a belief that the valued item is valuable, whereas that is not true of Cohen's category of personal value (and valuing). For him, something that has personal value need have no intrinsic value at all (p. 207). So although Cohen might well classify my kind of valuing as personal valuing, and although he might regard the conservative disposition as I describe it as deriving from features peculiar to that category, not everything that he would call personal valuing is an instance of valuing in my sense. To put it another way, valuing in my sense cuts across Cohen's categories of particular and personal valuing. It always includes both relational elements and a belief that the valued item is valuable. Neither "particular valuing" in the absence of any relational element nor "personal valuing" in the absence of a belief that the putatively valued item is valuable counts as an instance of valuing in my sense.

for the items she already valued in order to devote her efforts to creating new works of value. So conservatism as I understand it is not incompatible with creativity. This is important, because even if all sane people have something of the conservative disposition, all sane people also have something of the creative disposition. This disposition is not limited to artists or to others who are colloquially described as creative people. It reveals itself in the impulse to *make*, to *build*, to *invent*, to *change*, to *improve*, to *reform*, to *renew*, to *innovate*, and, of course, to *procreate*. It reveals itself even in the impulse to act, because each act is a novel intervention in the world; each act contributes something new to the course of human history. In that sense, the conservative disposition to sustain and preserve the things that we value is itself a creative disposition. To be sure, there are times when all it requires of us is that we refrain from performing actions that would harm or destroy those things, but there are also times when we must take affirmative steps, often requiring great imagination and tenacity, if we are to succeed in sustaining and preserving the things that we value. After all, conservators are not people whose job is simply to do nothing. The conservative disposition and the creative disposition are not incompatible, then, not only because there are cases in which one of them applies and the other doesn't but also because there is a sense in which the conservative disposition, properly understood, is itself a creative disposition.

This brings us back to the role of the conservative disposition in supporting our concern for the survival and flourishing of future generations. I have emphasized the extent to which our reasons to care about the fate of our successors are rooted in our value-based attachments to humanity and to the many different forms of human activity and endeavor that we cherish. Far from being a backward-looking impulse that competes with or inhibits a concern for the future of humanity, our conservative disposition to sustain and preserve the things that we value itself underwrites that concern. Nor does the fact that our concern for future generations depends on this conservative disposition mean that it is incompatible with our creative impulses. To see this, one has only to reflect on the creativity and imagination that will be required to overcome the challenges to human survival and secure the prospects of a decent future for our successors. Moreover, since human beings are an essentially creative species, whose history is a history of change, experimentation, and innovation, and who are always developing new modes of living and new dimensions of value, a concern to ensure the future of humanity is itself a concern to sustain the open-ended and unpredictable course of human creative activity. As applied to the future of humanity, in other words, the conservative disposition is a disposition to ensure that human creativity and innovation will continue to flourish.

Despite the ways in which the conservative disposition supports rather than competes with a concern for the future, skeptics may deny that the disposition is rational. Insofar as it gives existing valuable things priority over valuable things that do not yet exist, it may be said to amount to an irrational form of "status quo bias."[10] But although I am sure that there is such a thing as irrational status quo

---

[10] For a discussion of status quo bias and a proposed test for identifying and eliminating it, see Nick Bostrom and Toby Ord, "The Reversal Test: Eliminating Status Quo Bias in Applied Ethics," *Ethics* 116(2006): 656–79. In his article, Cohen asserts (p. 229, fn. 31) that the considerations adduced by Bostrom and Ord cannot be applied against his form of conservatism. However, in "Cohen's Conservatism and Human Enhancement," *Journal of Ethics* 17(2013): 331–54, at 338, fn. 13, Jonathan Pugh, Guy Kahane, and Julian Savulescu express skepticism about Cohen's ability to avoid the charge of status quo bias. Jacob Nebel, meanwhile, argues in "Status Quo Bias, Rationality, and Conservatism about Value," *Ethics* 125(2015): 449–76, that

bias, I have a difficult time seeing that there is anything irrational about the conservative disposition as I have described it. That is because I have a difficult time seeing what the alternative to it might be. The conservative disposition reflects the fact that, in general, our value-based attachments can be directed only at what is (or has been) actual. We could not have a temporally neutral disposition to form attachments to things that do not yet exist in the same way that we do to existing things. What would it mean to be just as attached to our future friends or to the children we will one day have or to the great paintings that will someday be produced or to the great novels that will someday be written as we are to our actual friends or children or to the great paintings and novels that have already been produced? When it comes to attachment, temporal neutrality is not an option.

An alternative suggestion might be that attachment is always irrational. We should strive to realize an ideal of *de*tachment and to free ourselves, as far as possible, from all of our attachments.[11] Whatever may be said for or against such an ideal of detachment, however, it does not support the idea that our bias toward existing attachments in particular is irrational. Instead, what is alleged to be irrational is attachment itself, rather than the temporal sensitivity of our disposition to form attachments. It is true that, if all attachments are irrational, then it follows trivially that a temporally sensitive pattern of attachments is irrational. But if all attachments are

---

Cohen's conservatism does manifest status quo bias but that, in so doing, it also shows why such bias need not be irrational.

[11] For a thought-provoking discussion of some of the issues raised by the ideal of detachment, see Sharon Street, "Constructivism in Ethics and the Problem of Attachment and Loss," *Proceedings of the Aristotelian Society Supplementary Volume* 90(2016): 161–89.

irrational, then it also follows trivially that a temporally neutral pattern of attachments would be irrational. The ideal of detachment does not show that there is anything irrational about temporal sensitivity per se.

In general, the interactions between our values and our attitudes toward time are complex, and we should be cautious about assuming that every manifestation of temporal bias in our valuing attitudes must be irrational. Indeed, to the extent that the very term "bias" suggests irrationality or lack of justification, its undiscriminating use to refer to all forms of temporal preference is unfortunate. Our values and desires are shaped by our self-understanding as temporally extended creatures and by our experience of temporality. We would not have the values we have if we did not understand the temporal dimension of our lives in the ways that we do. And the direction of influence also runs the other way. The values that we form serve in turn to shape our attitudes toward time. We would not have the temporal attitudes that we have if we did not have the values that we do. We need to try to understand these reciprocal influences and not to assume that every manifestation of temporal bias in our valuing attitudes is irrational. As with studies of rational judgment and decision-making in other areas, the trick is to navigate between the complacent assumption that our ordinary thinking must be in good order and the revisionist application of oversimplified models that lack any authority over our actual practices and tendencies of thought.

I have tried to illustrate these broad themes by showing how a conservative disposition to sustain existing bearers of value, which some might take to involve a form of irrational status quo bias, is built into our valuing attitudes and cooperates rather than competes with a concern for the future. This in turn helps to explain why, in the case that is the special focus of this book, the conservative disposition strongly supports a concern for the survival of humanity and the flourishing of future generations. To state my view in a way that is only superficially paradoxical, much of our concern for the *future* of humanity, and for the flourishing of *future* generations, depends on a conservative disposition that applies directly only to *presently* existing and *past* bearers of value. In the next section, I want to develop these ideas further, by considering the conservative disposition alongside other forms of temporal bias that we have been said to exhibit. This will enable us to see how a conservative concern for future generations fits within the broader context of the more general relations between our attitudes toward time and our attitudes toward value.

The bias toward the future and its limits

You awake in your hospital bed. You are told by a nurse that either you underwent ten hours of extremely painful surgery without anesthesia yesterday, after which you were given a drug to cause you to forget the experience, or else you will undergo one hour of extremely painful surgery without anesthesia today, after which you will be given a drug to cause you to forget the experience. Which would you prefer? Most of us would prefer to have undergone the longer operation yesterday than to be faced with the shorter operation today. Derek Parfit has deployed a well-known series of examples of this kind to argue that we display a bias toward the future in the following respects.[12] We would prefer to have experienced pain of a given intensity and duration in the past than to experience it in the future. We would even prefer to have experienced a longer period of pain in the past than to experience a

[12] See Parfit, *Reasons and Persons*, chapter 8.

shorter period of pain in the future. And we would prefer that our lives contain more total hours of pain, if that meant less of it were still to come.

Anthony Brueckner and John Martin Fischer have used an example parallel to one of Parfit's to argue that, with respect to pleasurable sensations, we have the reverse preferences.[13] We would prefer to experience pleasure of a given intensity and duration in the future than to have experienced it in the past. We would even prefer to experience a shorter period of pleasure in the future than to have experienced a longer period in the past. And we would prefer our lives to contain fewer total hours of pleasure, if that meant more of it were still to come. Taken together, and setting aside for the moment various refinements and qualifications, these claims ascribe to us a general preference that our pains be in the past and our pleasures in the future. With respect to pleasure and pain, we are, so to speak, more *solicitous* of our futures than of our pasts. In that sense, we are biased toward the future.

Parfit says that the bias toward the future is not the only form of temporal bias that we exhibit. Most of us, for example, also exhibit a bias toward the near. We would prefer a smaller pleasure sooner to a larger pleasure later, and a larger pain later to a smaller pain sooner. He also says that the bias toward the future is limited in scope. It is a feature of our attitudes toward certain of our *experiences*, but it is not a feature of our attitudes toward all the good and bad things in our lives. In the same vein, Brueckner and Fischer say that the bias does not apply to bad things that we do not experience.

[13] Anthony Brueckner and John Martin Fischer, "Why is Death Bad?," in Fischer, ed., *The Metaphysics of Death* (Stanford, CA: Stanford University Press, 1993), pp. 221–9.

For example, they hold that it would not apply to a case in which you knew that "either some friends of yours have betrayed you behind your back nine times in the past or some friend will betray you behind your back once in the future."[14] Here, in contrast to the examples involving the bad experience of pain, it is not true that most of us would prefer the larger number of betrayals as long as they were in the past.

Parfit adds that, "for simplicity,"[15] his examples focus solely on experiences of pleasure and pain. The phrase "for simplicity" suggests that, in his view, the bias toward the future also applies to other kinds of experiences. It is not clear what other kinds of experiences he has in mind. But there are many experiences to which the bias toward the future does not seem to apply with comparable force, if at all. Many of the good and bad things in our lives have an experiential dimension, and yet we do not regard their value as exhausted by the associated experiences. I regard my friendships as valuable, and they do have an experiential dimension, yet I do not think that their value for me consists solely in my experience of them. If I did, I would think it just as valuable if an "experience machine" could provide me with qualitatively identical experiences in the absence of any actual friendship.[16] Similarly, Jill regards her life as greatly enriched by creating good paintings, but she does not think that the value for her of creating the paintings consists solely

---

[14] Ibid., p. 225. See also Caspar Hare, "Time—The Emotional Asymmetry," in Heather Dyke and Adrian Bardon, eds., *A Companion to the Philosophy of Time* (John Wiley & Sons, Inc., 2013): pp. 507–20, esp. section 2.

[15] *Reasons and Persons*, p. 172.

[16] See Robert Nozick, *Anarchy, State, and Utopia* (New York: Basic Books, 1974), pp. 42–5.

in the experiences she has while doing so. What is important to her is that she actually creates the paintings, and not merely that she has certain states of mind while creating them.

A corresponding point applies to many bad things. If someone I love dies, then what is bad is not my grief but the person's death. If I know that my friend has betrayed me, or that someone has violated my rights, or that my life's work has turned out to be a failure, then the disvalue of these things for me consists in the fact that they have happened and not solely in my experience of them. To be sure, it would be bad to undergo experiences *as of* their happening, but it would be worse if, in addition, they really did happen.

We may call goods and bads of this kind *partly experiential*. With partly experiential goods and bads, we do not have a general bias toward the future. Would you prefer already to have painted five great paintings or to paint one such painting in the future? Would you prefer knowingly to have undergone five painless rights violations in the past or to undergo one such violation in the future? If our bias toward the future applied to these cases, we would prefer to paint one great painting in the future rather than to have painted five in the past, and to have undergone five painless rights violations in the past rather than to undergo one in the future. But it is far from clear that most people would have these preferences. Many would have the reverse preferences.[17,18]

---

[17] In "The Lucretian Argument," in R. Feldman, K. McDaniel, J.R. Raibley, and M.J. Zimmerman, eds., *The Good, the Right, Life and Death: Essays in Honor of Fred Feldman* (Aldershot, UK: Ashgate Publishing, 2006), pp. 213–26, Jeff McMahan uses an example modeled on Parfit's original cases to make a related point about achievement.

[18] It may be proposed that the reverse preferences in these cases are actually compatible with a bias toward the future. That is because partly

experiential goods and bads in the past can continue to be sources of desirable and undesirable experiences in the future. For example, the fact that we painted five great paintings in the past may be a source of pride and satisfaction in the future. Similarly, the fact that we underwent five painless rights violations in the past can be a source of anger and humiliation in the future. So both the preference to have painted five paintings in the past, rather than to paint one in future, and the preference to undergo one painless rights violation in the future, rather than to have undergone five such violations in the past, can be explained in ways that are compatible with the bias toward the future. In the first case, we judge that our awareness of our greater past accomplishments would lead to more favorable experiences in the future than would our (eventual) awareness of our more modest future accomplishment. And in the second case, we judge that our awareness of our greater past victimization would lead to more unfavorable experiences in the future than would our (eventual) awareness of our lesser future victimization. So our "reverse preferences"—to have painted five paintings in the past and to undergo one rights violation in the future— are at least compatible with (and may even manifest) a bias toward the future, that is, a desire to maximize favorable future experiences and to minimize unfavorable future experiences, even at the cost of failing to maximize total lifetime favorable experiences or to minimize total lifetime unfavorable experiences. But it is important to note that the favorable and unfavorable experiences that are cited in this argument—pride and satisfaction on the one hand and anger and humiliation on the other—are themselves responses to certain non-experiential facts: facts about our accomplishments in the one case and our mistreatment in the other. They presuppose that what is good or bad for us is what actually happened, and not just our experience of what happened. And our reverse preferences in these cases demonstrate, first, that we would rather have a larger number of those good things in the past than a smaller number in the future, and, second, that we would rather have a smaller number of those bad things in the future than a larger number in the past. This means that we have no bias toward the future with respect to these goods and bads. Moreover, many people might retain these preferences even if they knew that they

Parfit might agree. He says that he is "discussing our attitude, not to the *fact* that our lives contain certain kinds of event, but to our *experience* at other times of living through these events."[19] This comment is open to different interpretations. On one interpretation, it implies that he is not making any claim about temporal bias in the case of partly experiential goods and bads. If that is right, then there is no inconsistency between Parfit's position and what I have said about such goods and bads. On another interpretation, however, it implies that the claim of temporal bias applies only to the experiential dimension of partly experiential goods and bads, and not to their non-experiential dimensions. So, for example, the claim might be that our bias toward the future applies, not to facts about the deaths of our loved ones, but only to our experience of their deaths, for example grief. Or, similarly, the idea might be that the bias applies only to our experience of our friendships, and not to the friendships themselves.

Interpreted this way, the claim is untenable. Partly experiential goods and bads cannot be decomposed into two elements, toward one of which we exhibit the temporal bias and toward the other of which we do not. If they could be so decomposed, then we might, for example, be expected to have the following combination of preferences: a preference to have a smaller number of our close friends die in the near future rather than to have had a larger number

would subsequently have no awareness or memory of the goods and bads in question. For example, they might prefer to have painted five great paintings in the past, rather than to paint one in the future, even if they knew that, in either case, they would have no subsequent knowledge or memory of their accomplishment. These preferences appear incompatible with a bias toward the future.

[19] *Reasons and Persons*, p. 172.

die in the past, along with a preference to have experienced a larger number of episodes of grief about our friends' deaths in the past rather than to experience a smaller number of such episodes in the near future. But it is not clear that such a combination of preferences is even coherent, and there is in any event no basis for attributing it, or others like it, to us.

In the case of partly experiential goods and bads, our attitudes toward our experiences of these things are intimately bound up with our attitudes toward the facts or events of which they are experiences. That is why the bias toward the future does not, in general, apply to them. The fact that the bias does not apply to them does not entail either that we are temporally neutral with respect to all such goods and bads or that we exhibit toward all of them some other temporal bias of the kind that interests Parfit. What temporal preferences we have, if any, may depend instead on context and on the nature of the specific goods and bads that are in question. The bias toward the future, meanwhile, applies most obviously to pleasure and pain, where these are understood as pure feelings or sensations with little or no cognitive content, rather than as ways of experiencing events or aspects of the world that have independent value or disvalue for us. Even if we suppose that grief can sometimes be physically painful, for example, I would much prefer to have my grief at the loss of my friends lie in the future rather than in the past.[20] Beyond

---

[20] Of course, this preference might be subject to further examination and demands for refinement in the spirit of Parfit's hospital example. For reasons deriving precisely from the differences between simple pain and grief at the loss of a friend, however, it is difficult to construct convincing examples on the model of the hospital case to help probe this preference. Suffice it to say this: to the extent that I can make sense of the question, I would certainly not prefer to have experienced grief about the actual

the case of pleasure and pain understood as pure sensations, it is not clear how far the bias toward the future extends.[21]

There is at least one other important case in which we seem clearly to exhibit such a bias, however, and that is the case of personal non-existence. We are troubled by our future non-existence in a way that we are not troubled by our past non-existence. As Lucretius famously observed, our fear of death is not matched by any comparably strong dismay about the fact that we did not exist prior to our births. As with pain, we would prefer to have our non-existence in the past rather than in the future. And as with pleasure, we would prefer to have our existence in the future rather than in the past.

However, these assertions may need to be qualified in certain ways. It is true, of course, that many people fear death intensely, while nobody that I know of feels comparably strong dismay about his or her pre-natal non-existence.[22] But it may be too hasty to assert

---

deaths of five of my close friends in the recent past than to experience grief about the actual death of one such friend in the near future.

[21] For related discussion, see David Brink, "Prospects for Temporal Neutrality," in C. Callender, ed., *The Oxford Handbook of Philosophy of Time* (Oxford: Oxford University Press, 2011), pp. 352–81, at p. 378, and Hare, "Time—The Emotional Asymmetry."

[22] Consider, though, the striking opening passage of Nabokov's *Speak Memory*: "The cradle rocks above an abyss, and common sense tells us that our existence is but a brief crack of light between two eternities of darkness. Although the two are identical twins, man, as a rule, views the prenatal abyss with more calm than the one he is heading for (at some forty-five hundred heartbeats an hour). I know, however, of a young chronophobiac who experienced something like panic when looking for the first time at homemade movies that had been taken a few weeks before his birth. He saw a world that was practically

without qualification that we would prefer to have our non-existence in the past and our existence in the future. Suppose I were told that I could, *per impossibile*, trade the first forty years of my past existence for an additional forty years of future existence, during which time I would remain in good health and would retain my physical and mental powers, except that toward the end I would be subject to the normal aging process. If I had an unrestricted preference for past non-existence over future non-existence, then I would gladly accept the trade. But since, in losing the first forty years of my actual existence, I would lose much of the personal history that I value most dearly, including all of my relationships with people I met during those years, I would not accept the trade. I would not accept it even if I were assured that I would establish new relationships in the future that I would eventually come to value just as much as, or even more than, I now value the relationships I would be losing. And this shows that I do not have an unrestricted or unqualified preference for past non-existence over future non-existence. Other people might make different choices in the situation I have described, especially if, for example, they had formed only weak relationships in the first decades of their lives. But as long as there are some people who would refuse the trade, it follows that our general bias toward the future with respect to our own existence is not as

unchanged—the same house, the same people—and then realized that he did not exist there at all and that nobody mourned his absence. He caught a glimpse of his mother waving from an upstairs window, and that unfamiliar gesture disturbed him, as if it were some mysterious farewell. But what particularly frightened him was the sight of a brand-new baby carriage standing there on the porch, with the smug, encroaching air of a coffin; even that was empty, as if, in the reverse course of events, his very bones had disintegrated" (New York: Vintage International Edition, 1989, p. 19).

unrestricted as it may have seemed. In particular, it can be limited by past attachments. Even if we fear death but remain indifferent to our actual pre-natal non-existence, we might nevertheless prefer to retain our actual past existence, and the attachments that came with it, rather than accept additional past non-existence in exchange for additional future existence.[23]

The picture that has begun to emerge suggests that our attitudes toward time and value form a complex network. We exhibit no global temporal neutrality, but neither do we exhibit a comprehensive bias toward either the past or the future. In part, we have a conservative disposition, because it follows from the nature of attachment that valuable things that already exist are reason-giving for us in a way that future valuable things are not. Yet this disposition coexists with an equally pronounced creative disposition. We also display a bias toward the future with regard to our purely pleasurable and purely painful sensations, but this bias does not apply to all of the good and bad things in our lives. And although we fear death intensely but remain generally indifferent to pre-natal non-existence, we do not have an unrestricted or unqualified preference for past non-existence over future non-existence.

It is evident that these preferences and dispositions interact with one another in a variety of ways. For example, the fact that

---

[23] In "The Lucretian Argument," Jeff McMahan appeals to the significance of personal attachments, in a similar spirit, to explain why one might not regret that one did not come into existence earlier even if an earlier starting point would have meant that one's life was longer. Other important discussions of the significance of personal attachments in shaping one's retrospective attitudes toward one's past include Robert Adams, "Existence, Self-Interest, and the Problem of Evil," Kieran Setiya, "Retrospection," and R. Jay Wallace, *The View from Here* (New York: Oxford University Press, 2013).

our existing attachments are reason-giving for us in a way that our future attachments are not helps to explain why our preference for past non-existence over future non-existence is limited. Similarly, the reason-giving force of our existing attachments helps to explain why the bias toward the future that we exhibit with respect to our sensations of pleasure and pain does not extend to all the good and bad things in our lives. To provide a complete map of our attitudes toward time and value would be a substantial project, and one that I cannot undertake here. But even without a complete map in hand, it may be helpful to situate questions about future generations in the context of this broader set of issues, and that is what I will attempt to do, albeit briefly, by way of conclusion.

Thinking about future generations: contrasting perspectives revisited

In his discussion of our bias toward the future, Parfit highlights the question of whether the bias is irrational and whether rationality requires complete temporal neutrality. He stops short of explicitly endorsing this position, although he does say that the bias is bad for us, and that it would be better for us if we lacked it.[24] I am not convinced that he is right about that, although I will not explore my doubts in any detail here. Suffice it to say that I am not convinced that he has taken adequate account of the effects that temporal neutralism, even if limited to pleasure and pain and to existence and

---

[24] Brueckner and Fischer ("Why is Death Bad?," pp. 223–4) nevertheless interpret him as thinking that the bias toward the future is *not* irrational. However, Parfit himself said subsequently that he did mean to be endorsing the view that the bias is irrational but that he made this insufficiently clear (personal communication, September 26, 2015).

non-existence, would have on the rest of our values and attachments. And although I have emphasized the limits of our bias toward the future, I am skeptical of the neutralist claim that rationality requires us to eliminate or overcome it entirely.[25] I believe this is one of those cases in which, when confronted with the complexity of our actual thought, we should be wary of the prescriptive application of a simplified model of rationality that would classify any recalcitrant attitudes as being normatively deficient.

There is, of course, a well-known parallel between the view that temporal neutrality is the default rational stance, departures from which stand in need of special justification, and the view that impartial beneficence is the default moral stance, departures from which stand in need of special justification.[26] The first view treats temporal neutralism as presumptively authoritative, and is suspicious of any tendency people may have to be more concerned about what happens at some times than at others. The second view treats an equal concern for the welfare of all people as the presumptively authoritative moral position, and is suspicious of any tendency people may have to attach special value to their relationships with particular people or to be more concerned about what happens to some people than to others.

---

[25] For arguments that the bias is irrational, see David Brink, "Prospects for Temporal Neutrality"; Tom Dougherty, "Future Bias and Practical Reason," *Philosophers' Imprint* 15(2015): 1–16; and Preston Greene and Meghan Sullivan, "Against Time Bias," *Ethics* 125(2015): 1–24.

[26] This parallel is taken to form the basis for a possible objection to rational egoism by Sidgwick in *The Methods of Ethics*, pp. 418–19, and it plays a central role in Parfit's arguments against the "self-interest theory" in *Reasons and Persons*. See also Thomas Nagel, *The Possibility of Altruism* (New York: Oxford University Press, 1970).

I reject both of these views. I am comfortable with the thought that our temporal attitudes are complex and that we lack any single master attitude toward time: that we are not uniformly biased toward the past, uniformly biased toward the future, or uniformly neutral. I am also comfortable with the thought that we have strong value-laden attachments to particular people and projects and relationships, and that these attachments are sources of differential reasons for action and differential forms of emotional vulnerability.

This bears on the contrast that I drew in Chapter Four between two different ways of thinking about questions concerning future generations. As applied to those questions, the combination of temporal and moral neutralism leads more or less directly to the quest for a principle of beneficence that would solve the puzzles of population ethics. At first glance, such a principle might seem to be the perfect antidote to the kind of temporal parochialism that I discussed in Chapter One. But as I have tried to make clear throughout this book, I believe that this solution is illusory, and that once one focuses on the rich variety of human values and attachments and on the complexity of our actual attitudes toward time, many of which are still not well-understood, it begins to lose its charms.

It is tempting to think that, once that happens, our reasons for concerning ourselves with the fate of future generations simply drain away. Much of the beneficence-based literature tacitly, though no doubt unwittingly, encourages this thought. In this book, however, I have tried to show that the reverse is true. Once we free ourselves from the thought that the basis for any concern about the future of humanity must lie in a general principle of beneficence of some as yet unspecified sort, we can see that we have reasons of a number of different kinds, most of which are rooted in our actual attachments as flesh-and-blood human beings, for wanting future generations to survive and to flourish. Insofar as these reasons depend on our existing values and attachments and on our conservatism about value, they depart from moral and temporal neutralism. Yet it is to those very departures, rather than to any form of neutralist beneficence, that we must look in order to identify some of our strongest and deepest reasons for caring about the fate of our successors. Or so I have been trying to show. At the very least, I hope to have persuaded you that there is an alternative to thinking about problems of future generations in exclusively or primarily beneficence-based terms or, indeed, in exclusively moral terms of any kind. If we broaden our horizons, we may find that we have even more reasons than we realized to worry about the fate of future generations.

BIBLIOGRAPHY

Adams, Robert, "Existence, Self-Interest, and the Problem of Evil," *Noûs* 13(1979): 53–65.

Anderson, Elizabeth, *Value in Ethics and Economics* (Cambridge, MA: Harvard University Press, 1993).

Arrhenius, Gustaf, "An Impossibility Theorem for Welfarist Axiologies," *Economics and Philosophy* 16(2000): 247–66.

Arrhenius, Gustaf, "Can the Person-Affecting Restriction Solve the Problems in Population Ethics?," in Melinda A. Roberts and David T. Wasserman, eds., *Harming Future Persons* (Dordrecht: Springer Verlag, 2009), pp. 289–314.

Bader, Ralf, "Review of Cohen, *Finding Oneself in the Other*," *Notre Dame Philosophical Reviews* (April, 2013).

Barry, Brian, "Justice Between Generations," in P.M.S. Hacker and J. Raz, eds., *Law, Morality and Society: Essays in Honour of H.L.A. Hart* (Oxford: Clarendon Press, 1977), pp. 268–84.

Beitz, Charles, "Cicero on Justice and Beneficence," unpublished draft of August 17, 2015.

Benatar, David, *Better Never to Have Been* (Oxford: Clarendon Press, 2006).

Bennett, Jonathan, "On Maximizing Happiness," in R.I. Sikora and B. Barry, eds., *Obligations to Future Generations* (Philadelphia, PA: Temple University Press, 1978), pp. 61–73.

Birnbacher, Dieter, "What Motivates Us to Care for the (Distant) Future?," in Gosseries and Meyer, eds., *Intergenerational Justice* (Oxford: Oxford University Press, 2009), pp. 273–300.

Boonin, David, *The Non-Identity Problem and the Ethics of Future People* (Oxford: Oxford University Press, 2014).

Bostrom, Nick and Toby Ord, "The Reversal Test: Eliminating Status Quo Bias in Applied Ethics," *Ethics* 116(2006): 656–79.

Bowlby, John, *Attachment and Loss*, 3 vols. (New York: Basic Books, 1969–1980).

Brink, David, "Prospects for Temporal Neutrality," in C. Callender, ed., *The Oxford Handbook of Philosophy of Time* (Oxford: Oxford University Press, 2011), pp. 352–81.

Broome, John, *Climate Matters* (New York: W.W. Norton & Co., 2012).

Brueckner, Anthony and John Martin Fischer, "Why is Death Bad?," in J.M. Fischer, ed., *The Metaphysics of Death* (Stanford, CA: Stanford University Press, 1993), pp. 221–9.

Cohen, G.A., "Rescuing Conservatism: A Defense of Existing Value," in R.J. Wallace, R. Kumar, and S. Freeman, eds., *Reasons and Recognition: Essays on the Philosophy of T.M. Scanlon* (New York: Oxford University Press, 2011), pp. 203–30.

Cohen, G.A., *Finding Oneself in the Other*, edited by Michael Otsuka (Princeton, NJ: Princeton University Press, 2012).

Cohen, Joshua and Charles Sabel, "Extra Rempublicam Nulla Justitia?," *Philosophy & Public Affairs* 34(2006): 147–75.

Coscarelli, Joe, "The Artist Providing the Canvas for Kanye West's 'Famous' Video," *The New York Times*, June 29, 2016.

Davenport, Coral, "Optimism Faces Grave Realities at Climate Talks," *The New York Times*, December 1, 2014.

Dougherty, Tom, "Future Bias and Practical Reason," *Philosophers' Imprint* 15(2015): 1–16.

Eliot, T.S., *What is a Classic?* (London: Faber and Faber, 1944).

English, Jane, "Justice Between Generations," *Philosophical Studies* 31(1977): 91–104.

Foot, Philippa, "Utilitarianism and the Virtues," *Mind* 94(1985): 196–209.

Frankfurt, Harry, *The Reasons of Love* (Princeton, NJ: Princeton University Press, 2004).

Freeman, Samuel, *Rawls* (Abingdon: Routledge, 2007).

Frick, Johann, "On the Survival of Humanity," *Canadian Journal of Philosophy* 47 (2017): 344–67.

Gardiner, Stephen, *A Perfect Moral Storm: The Ethical Tragedy of Climate Change* (New York: Oxford University Press, 2011).

Gosseries, Axel, "Three Models of Intergenerational Reciprocity," in A. Gosseries and L. Meyer, eds., *Intergenerational Justice* (Oxford: Oxford University Press, 2009), pp. 119–46.

Gosseries, Axel and Lukas Meyer, eds., *Intergenerational Justice* (Oxford: Oxford University Press, 2009).

Greaves, Hilary, "Population Axiology," *Philosophy Compass* 12(2017), 12:e12442.

Greene, Preston and Meghan Sullivan, "Against Time Bias," *Ethics* 125(2015): 1–24.

Hare, Caspar, "Time—The Emotional Asymmetry," in Heather Dyke and Adrian Bardon, eds., *A Companion to the Philosophy of Time* (John Wiley & Sons, Inc., 2013): pp. 507–20.

Hauser, Oliver P., David G. Rand, Alexander Peysakhovich, and Martin A. Nowak, "Cooperating with the Future," *Nature* 511(July 10, 2014): 220–3.

Heath, Joseph, "The Structure of Intergenerational Cooperation," *Philosophy & Public Affairs* 41(2013): 31–66.

Hume, David. *Enquiry Concerning the Principles of Morals.*

James, P.D., *The Children of Men* (London: Faber and Faber, 1992).

Jamieson, Dale, *Reason in a Dark Time* (New York: Oxford University Press, 2014).

Jefferson, Thomas, *The Papers of Thomas Jefferson*, ed. Julian Boyd, Volume 15 (Princeton, NJ: Princeton University Press, 1958).

Kolodny, Niko, "Love as Valuing a Relationship," *Philosophical Review* 112(2003): 135–89.

Kumar, Rahul, "Who Can Be Wronged?," *Philosophy & Public Affairs* 31(2003): 99–118.

Kumar, Rahul, "Wronging Future People: A Contractualist Proposal," in A. Gosseries and L. Meyer, eds., *Intergenerational Justice* (Oxford: Oxford University Press, 2009), pp. 251–72.

Lenman, James, "On Becoming Extinct," *Pacific Philosophical Quarterly* 83(2002): 253–69.

McCarthy, Cormac, *The Road* (New York: Vintage Books, 2006).

McMahan, Jeff, "The Lucretian Argument," in R. Feldman, K. McDaniel, J.R. Raibley, and M.J. Zimmerman, eds., *The Good, the Right, Life and Death: Essays in Honor of Fred Feldman* (Aldershot, UK: Ashgate Publishing, 2006), pp. 213–26.

Misak, Cheryl, *Cambridge Pragmatism: From Peirce and James to Ramsey and Wittgenstein* (Oxford: Oxford University Press, 2016).

Nabokov, V., *Speak Memory* (New York: Vintage International Edition, 1989).

Nagel, Thomas, *The Possibility of Altruism* (New York: Oxford University Press, 1970).

Narveson, Jan, "Utilitarianism and New Generations," *Mind* 76(1967): 62–72.

Narveson, Jan, "Moral Problems of Population," *The Monist* 57(1973): 62–86.

Narveson, Jan, "Future People and Us," in R.I. Sikora and B. Barry, eds., *Obligations to Future Generations* (Philadelphia, PA: Temple University Press, 1978), pp. 38–60.

Nebel, Jacob, "Status Quo Bias, Rationality, and Conservatism about Value," *Ethics* 125(2015): 449–76.

Nozick, Robert, *Anarchy, State, and Utopia* (New York: Basic Books, 1974).

Nussbaum, Martha, "Duties of Justice, Duties of Material Aid: Cicero's Problematic Legacy," *Journal of Political Philosophy* 8(2000): 176–206.

Owens, David, "Review of Scheffler, *Death and the Afterlife*," *The Times Literary Supplement* (February 21, 2014): 21.

Parfit, Derek, *Reasons and Persons* (Oxford: Clarendon Press, 1984).

Parfit, Derek, *On What Matters* (Oxford: Oxford University Press, 2011).

Parfit, Derek, "Can We Avoid the Repugnant Conclusion?," *Theoria* 82(2016): 110–17.

Pugh, Jonathan, Guy Kahane, and Julian Savulescu, "Cohen's Conservatism and Human Enhancement," *Journal of Ethics* 17(2013): 331–54.

Rawls, John, *A Theory of Justice* (Cambridge, MA: Harvard University Press, 1971; revised edition, 1999).

Rawls, John, *Political Liberalism* (New York: Columbia University Press, 1993).

Rawls, John, *Justice as Fairness: A Restatement* (Cambridge, MA: Harvard University Press, 2001).

Roberts, M.A., "Population Axiology," in I. Hirose and J. Olson, eds., *The Oxford Handbook of Value Theory* (New York: Oxford University Press, 2015), pp. 399–423.

Ross, W.D., *The Right and the Good* (Oxford: Clarendon Press, 1930; rev. ed. 2002).

Rubenfeld, Jed, *Freedom and Time* (New Haven, CT: Yale University Press, 2001).

Russell, Bertrand, "Knowledge by Acquaintance and Knowledge by Description," *Proceedings of the Aristotelian Society* 11 (1910–11): 108–28.

Scanlon, T.M., *What We Owe to Each Other* (Cambridge, MA: Harvard University Press, 1998).

Scheffler, Samuel, "Agent-Centered Restrictions, Rationality, and the Virtues," *Mind* 94(1985): 409–19.

Scheffler, Samuel, *Boundaries and Allegiances* (Oxford: Oxford University Press, 2001).

Scheffler, Samuel, "Projects, Relationships, and Reasons," in R. Jay Wallace, Philip Pettit, Samuel Scheffler, and Michael Smith, eds., *Reason and Value: Themes from the Moral Philosophy of Joseph Raz* (Oxford: Clarendon Press, 2004), pp. 247–69.

Scheffler, Samuel, "Immigration and the Significance of Culture," *Philosophy & Public Affairs* 35(2007): 93–125, reprinted in *Equality and Tradition* (New York: Oxford University Press, 2010), pp. 256–86.

Scheffler, Samuel, *Equality and Tradition* (New York: Oxford University Press, 2010).

Scheffler, Samuel, "Valuing," in *Equality and Tradition* (New York: Oxford University Press, 2010), pp. 15–40.

Scheffler, Samuel, "The Normativity of Tradition," in *Equality and Tradition* (New York: Oxford University Press, 2010), pp. 287–311.

Scheffler, Samuel, *Death and the Afterlife* (New York: Oxford University Press, 2013).

Schell, Jonathan, *The Fate of the Earth* (New York: Alfred A. Knopf, 1982).

Schelling, Thomas, "Intergenerational and International Discounting," *Risk Analysis* 20(2000): 833–7.

Scruton, Roger, *How to Think Seriously about the Planet: The Case for Environmental Conservatism* (New York: Oxford University Press, 2012).

Setiya, Kieran, "Retrospection," *Philosophers' Imprint* 16, No. 15(August, 2015).

Setiya, Kieran, "Ignorance, Beneficence, and Rights" (unpublished draft).

Setiya, Kieran, "Other People" (unpublished draft).

Shiffrin, Seana, "Preserving the Valued or Preserving Valuing?," in Samuel Scheffler, *Death and the Afterlife* (New York: Oxford University Press, 2013), pp. 143–58.

Shue, Henry, *Climate Justice* (New York: Oxford University Press, 2014).

Shute, Nevil, *On the Beach* (Heinemann, 1958).

Sider, Ted, *Four Dimensionalism* (Oxford: Clarendon Press, 2001).

Sidgwick, Henry, *The Methods of Ethics*, 7th edition (Macmillan & Co., 1907; republished by Hackett Publishing Company, Indianapolis, 1981).

Srinivasan, Amia, "Review of Scheffler, *Death and the Afterlife*," *London Review of Books* (September 25, 2014): 13–14.

Street, Sharon, "Constructivism in Ethics and the Problem of Attachment and Loss," *Proceedings of the Aristotelian Society Supplementary Volume* 90(2016): 161–89.

Sumner, Wayne, "Classical Utilitarianism and the Population Optimum," in R.I. Sikora and B. Barry, eds., *Obligations to Future Generations* (Philadelphia, PA: Temple University Press, 1978), pp. 91–111.

Tännsjö, Torbjörn, *Conservatism for Our Time* (London: Routledge, 1990).

Temkin, Larry, "Rationality with Respect to People, Places, and Times," *Canadian Journal of Philosophy* 45(2016): 576–608.

Thompson, Dennis, "Representing Future Generations: Political Presentism and Democratic Trusteeship," *Critical Review of International Social and Political Philosophy* 13(2010): 17–37.

Thompson, Janna, *Intergenerational Justice* (New York: Routledge, 2009).

Thomson, Judith Jarvis, "The Right and the Good," *Journal of Philosophy* 94(1997): 273–98.

Thomson, Judith Jarvis, *Goodness and Advice*, ed. Amy Gutmann (Princeton, NJ: Princeton University Press, 2001).

Wallace, R. Jay, *The View from Here* (New York: Oxford University Press, 2013).

Wallace, R. Jay, "Value, Trauma, and the Future of Humanity," unpublished.

Wells, Thomas, "Votes for the Future," *Aeon*, May 8, 2014.

Williams, Bernard, *Shame and Necessity* (Berkeley: University of California Press, 1993).

Winters, Ben H., *The Last Policeman* (Philadelphia, PA: Quirk Books, 2012).

Wolf, Susan, *Meaning in Life and Why It Matters* (Princeton, NJ: Princeton University Press, 2010).

Wood, Allen, *Fichte's Ethical Thought* (Oxford: Oxford University Press, 2016).

Woodward, James, "The Non-Identity Problem," *Ethics* 96(1986): 804–31.

INDEX

Adams, Robert 107n, 131n
Ainsworth, Mary 88n
Anderson, Elizabeth 63n
Arrhenius, Gustaf 28n, 94n

Bader, Ralf 113n
Barry, Brian 16–17, 21n, 72n
Beitz, Charles 30n
Benatar, David 39n
Bennett, Jonathan 34n
Birnbacher, Dieter 35n
Boonin, David 78n
Bostrom, Nick 119n
Bowlby, John 88n
Brink, David 129n, 133n
Broome, John 12n, 14n
Brueckner, Anthony 123–4, 132n

Caney, Simon 14n
Cicero 30n
Cohen, G.A. 105–14, 116–17
Cohen, Joshua 8n
Coscarelli, Joe 52n

Davenport, Coral 12n
Desiderio, Vincent 52
Dougherty, Tom 133n

Eliot, T.S. 4
English, Jane 21n

Fichte, Johann Gottlieb 41n
Fischer, John Martin 123–4, 132n
Foley, Duncan 12n
Foot, Philippa 32n
Frankfurt, Harry 65n
Freeman, Samuel 71, 74
Frick, Johann 103n

Gardiner, Stephen 14n
Gheaus, Anca 112
Gosseries, Axel 71n
Greaves, Hilary 94
Greene, Preston 133n

Hare, Caspar 124n, 129n
Hauser, Oliver 83n
Heath, Joseph 71n
Heidegger, Martin 41n
Hume, David 57n

James, P.D. 41–2
Jamieson, Dale 13n, 14n
Jefferson, Thomas 6n, 9

Kahane, Guy 119n
King, Martin Luther, Jr. 47n
Kolodny, Niko 62n
Kumar, Rahul 25n

Lenman, James 34n
Levinas, Emmanuel 41n
Lewis, David 4n
Lucretius 129

McCarthy, Cormac 42n, 44n
McMahan, Jeff 125n, 131n
Madison, James 6n
Major, John 108
Misak, Cheryl 41n

Nabokov, Vladimir 129–30n
Nagel, Thomas 21n, 133n
Narveson, Jan 27–8n
Nebel, Jacob 119n
Nowak, Martin A. 83n
Nozick, Robert 124n
Nussbaum, Martha 30n

Ord, Toby 119n
Orwell, George 108n
Otsuka, Michael 106n, 109
Owens, David 54n

Parfit, Derek 21–2, 24, 28–30, 78, 84–5, 95, 122–4, 127–8, 132, 133n
Peysakhovich, Alexander 83n
Pugh, Jonathan 119n

Ramakrishnan, Ketan 116n
Rand, David 83n
Rawls, John 20–1, 24, 36, 65n, 76, 79
Roberts, M.A. 28n
Ross, W.D. 31n
Rubenfeld, Jed 7n
Russell, Bertrand 115n

Sabel, Charles 8n
Savulescu, Julian 119n
Scanlon, T.M. 25n, 99n
Schell, Jonathan 42n, 43n
Schelling, Thomas 13n
Scruton, Roger 34n, 80n
Setiya, Kieran 115n, 131n
Shakespeare, William 99n

Shiffrin, Seana 69, 70n
Shue, Henry 14n
Shute, Nevil 42n
Sider, Ted 7n
Sidgwick, Henry 27n, 133n
Srinivasan, Amia 54n
Street, Sharon 120n
Sullivan, Meghan 133n
Sumner, Wayne 27n

Tännsjö, Torbjörn 91n
Temkin, Larry 12n, 95
Thompson, Dennis 83n
Thompson, Janna 53n
Thomson, Judith 32n
von Trier, Lars 42n
Trump, Donald 10n

Wallace, R. Jay 45–6n, 57n, 70n, 131n
Wells, Thomas 83n
West, Kanye 52
Williams, Bernard 4n
Winters, Ben H. 42n
Wolf, Susan 65n
Wood, Allen 41n
Woodward, James 32n